Tailoring a Jacket

Tailoring a Jacket

Gill McBride

The Crowood Press

First published in 2020 by
The Crowood Press Ltd
Ramsbury, Marlborough
Wiltshire SN8 2HR

enquiries@crowood.com
www.crowood.com

British Library Cataloguing-in-Publication Data

A catalogue record for this book is available from the British Library.

ISBN 978 1 78500 783 5

Typeset by Sharon Dainton
Printed and bound in India by Replika Press Pvt. Ltd.

CONTENTS

A, B

A

A

INTRODUCTION

Having a really good jacket in your wardrobe is almost essential! A jacket should be a staple in the wardrobe, ready to be worn with jeans for a lunch or a shopping trip or paired with some fabulous evening trousers or floaty skirt for a dinner date. A jacket is so versatile and it will make you feel well dressed and confident. Everyone needs at least one jacket in their wardrobe!

Jackets come in all shapes and sizes. Many have lapels or revers like a traditional gentleman's jacket but many do not. Jackets can be collarless, fitted, boxy, long, short, structured or unstructured. The fabric choice we now have is also endless. Whereas, traditionally, jackets would have been more structured or tailored and made from wool or silk fabrics, we can now make jackets from any fabric we choose, including sweatshirt fabrics and knitted fabrics.

The thought of making a jacket is exciting and daunting at the same time. In the past, tailoring a jacket was something that only specialist sewers would have attempted. Today, however, we have the tools and the fabrics to allow all of us to have a go at making a beautiful jacket that we are proud to wear.

This book will help you to make a jacket by the speed tailoring method, resulting in a garment that looks couture but does not take couture time to make.

GETTING STARTED

What is it that makes you love a jacket? It may be the colour or the fabric from which it is made. It may be that it moves from smart to casual really easily. It may be that it fits you really well. Whatever it is, look at the jackets that you have in your wardrobe and take out your favourite. Examine it and decide what it is that you particularly love about that jacket. Is it the princess seams that make it fit so well? Perhaps the length is just perfect for you. Maybe the simplicity or the details are what make the difference. Take a note of what exactly you love about that jacket and use those notes when looking for a pattern.

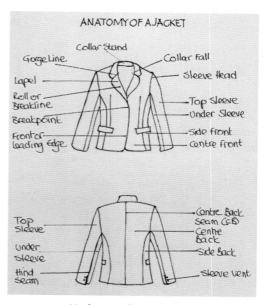

Understanding a jacket.

Understanding Your Jacket Before You Start

In the diagram here, you will see described the different parts of the jacket. There are some definitions that may be new to you and it will help you to understand these better. The particular ones to note are around the collar and lapel or rever area. For instance, the gorge line is the stitched line between the collar and the lapel/rever and is maybe the most worrying bit for us when we are new to sewing a jacket.

The roll line is exactly where the collar folds over down the front of the jacket. It is important to understand what the roll line is when we come to prepare the jacket pieces before sewing. The break point is the point where the collar roll stops on the front of the jacket and the jacket front lies flat again, ready for buttons and/or closures.

The collar stand is at the back of the collar and lies against the neck. The part of the collar that folds over is called the collar fall.

The sleeve head is the top part of the sleeve from the shoulder to mid-way to the elbow. On the flat pattern piece, the sleeve head is round the top of the armhole part of the sleeve pattern. This is also sometimes called the sleeve cap.

The leading edge is literally the front edge of the jacket, from below the break point to the hem.

The other definitions on the diagram are more self-explanatory, such as pocket flap, top sleeve and undersleeve, side front and so on. These are also usually named on the pattern pieces whereas the definitions above are not found on the pattern pieces because they only apply once the jacket is being put together.

Line drawings on back of pattern envelope, describing construction details.

Choosing Your Jacket Pattern

There are very many jacket styles to choose from and we each have our own favourite. Some of us will return to the blazer style with lapels and pockets. Some prefer a Chanel-style jacket that is very simple in design and where the fabric is the key factor. Casual jackets are also favoured by many and these can be lined or unlined, buttoned or zipped, short or long, structured or unstructured.

Choosing your style is important. It will make the world of a difference to the final garment if it is right for you. A princess-seamed jacket lies extremely well on all wearers, whatever their bust size. (Princess seams are long and curved and give a figure-hugging fit to the garment, especially over and below the bust.) Jackets with straight darts are easier for some of us to manage. Shorter jackets look good on all ages, if the fit is right. Longer-line jackets must be well fitted to look good and not 'drown' the wearer.

When looking for your jacket pattern, do not be influenced by the finishes that you see on the front of your chosen pattern envelope. Look at the lines of the jacket, its design, the way it is made, the dimensions, whether it has darts or not, whether it has princess seams or not, and whether the sleeves are one-piece or two-piece. The finishes such as buttonholes, pockets and even vents can be added or changed to suit your preferences; these are the features that you

can amend to make yours a one-off designer garment. The important features to look for in the pattern are the design and construction features to ensure that they are what you actually want to make and that they are what best suits you and your figure type.

Choosing Your Fabric

Fabric choice is as important as your style of pattern. However, fabric choice is also mostly influenced by what you want your jacket for. If you are making a Chanel-style jacket for smart or evening wear, you might want to use a fabulous tweed in a gorgeous colour with a co-ordinating trim or a fabulous brocade. However, if you want to make a Chanel-style jacket to wear informally with your jeans, you might choose a more casual fabric such as a jersey that you can quilt and line with some fun fabric.

The same applies for a blazer-type jacket. If you want to make an evening jacket, there is a wonderful array of fabric choices you can use and you can team them with amazing buttons, beautiful trims, fabulous linings and so on to make a stunning statement jacket. A blazer to wear to work, however, might need a more formal fabric that is practical in colour and will wear well and clean easily. A linen blazer will look wonderful on holiday with palazzo pants but might not look so tidy in the office. A blazer made with sweatshirt fabric and unlined is a great quick make for everyday wear.

Fabric choice is everything! We have at our fingertips a wealth of choice. There are tweeds, silks, velvets, twills, denims, cottons, linens and lots more besides. Nowadays a lot of these fabrics have an element of stretch in them and they sew really satisfactorily. Many of them work extremely well for a tailored garment as they can be interfaced with fusible (ironed-on) interfacing in the same way as a totally stable fabric. With confidence, we can use whatever fabric we like to make our jacket, if it is what we want to use. Remember though, if you are buying online, to make sure you get a sample first. Whether buying online or in a shop, test your chosen fabric to make sure it does not crush too much or stretch too much for what you want to make. Does it drape well? Will it hold its shape? If it has stripes or checks, will you be able to match them well enough? In other words, does the fabric work for the jacket you want to make?

Finally, test press your fabric to see how it responds to the iron, whether it needs a water spray or a damp cloth and to ascertain exactly the best way to press as you sew. It may be that when pressed, seams begin to show on the right side of the fabric, or the fabric does not press well with a dry iron. Decide how to get the best result from pressing before you begin sewing and practise using a tailor's ham and sleeve roll, if you have one or both to hand. They can make a huge difference to pressing your seams out and are described later in this chapter under 'Pressing Equipment'.

Choosing Your Lining – If You Need It

After you have chosen your fabric and if your jacket is to be lined, then you must now choose your lining. This is where you have another great opportunity to express yourself if you wish. A wonderfully contrasting lining can look

Tweed jacket with contrasting lining.

amazing inside a more simply styled jacket. For example, you could use a gorgeous simple tweed for your jacket and then line it with a heavily patterned lining fabric! It will look really striking when your jacket falls open and will give it another dimension. If your jacket is more complex in style you might feel that a contrast lining would detract from the design features of the jacket and a more stylish and formal lining would be more appropriate. Or you may prefer something simple inside that does not clash with what you will be wearing under the jacket. Again, with linings there is a huge choice of fabric. They may be plain, patterned or anti-static; they may be made of satin, cotton or a mixture of fibres. Some are cheaper than others and some will sew better than others, but you can also use any lightweight fabric that you love so long as you think it will work with your chosen jacket fabric and style.

Before you finally choose your lining, see how it works against your jacket fabric. Does it colour-match or contrast well? Will you be happy pattern-matching a striped lining? Is it the right weight – that is, is it too light or too heavy? Does it drape well? Does it crush or stretch and if so, will that be a problem? If it is cotton, will it stick to your clothes and will you be able to get the jacket on and off easily? A cotton lining is comfortable to wear but if you are wearing a cotton shirt or top underneath, then slipping your jacket on and off may become a nuisance as the lining of the jacket and the sleeves of your top will rub together.

Make your choice carefully as you did with your jacket fabric. All these choices will make a huge difference to the end product. They will all have an impact on your final garment and you want to be happy, proud and comfortable wearing your new jacket.

Everything Else You Will Need

So now you have chosen your pattern, your fabric and your lining. What else do you need to make your perfect jacket? Below is a list of sewing notions that will turn your jacket from a satisfactory garment into one that is beautifully finished and looks truly tailored.

Interfacing

This is a stabilizing fabric that is used on the wrong side of your garment fabric and helps to give your garment fabric body and structure. Interfacing can be fusible, meaning that it irons on, or non-fusible, meaning that it needs to be sewn in. Fusible or iron-on interfacing basically has a light surface of glue on one side of it; when you use the iron over it, applying the glue side on the wrong side of your fabric, the glue melts and adheres to your fabric. Sew-in interfacing is the same fabric but without the glue, and it has to be stitched into the garment seams to fix it. Nowadays, most interfacings are fusible.

Interfacings come in several weights and can be used on most fabrics, from the lightest to the heaviest. They will change the way a fabric feels, the way it hangs and the way it sews, so it is important to choose your weight of interfacing carefully. For your jacket you will need a mediumweight interfacing and a lightweight interfacing, both fusible.

TIP FOR INTERFACING

Be careful when choosing your interfacing. Do not be tempted to use one that makes your jacket fabric too stiff. It is surprising how 'a little goes a long way' in sewing and a slightly lighter-weight interfacing should work really well.

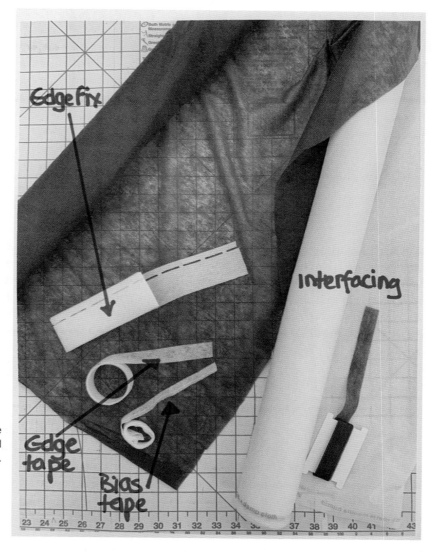

Interfacings, edge tape, bias tape and Edgefix.

Interfacing comes in three main colour groups that are readily available: white, cream/natural and black/charcoal. You may be able to find other colours for specific uses. Choose your colour according to your fabric and remember that if you are using a very lightweight fabric for your jacket in a pale colour, then a dark interfacing might change the look of your jacket fabric.

As there is so much choice of interfacing, you might want to sample a few different weights until you find the one that gives you the best feel for your fabric. Always test first and be careful not to use too heavy an interfacing or your fabric may become too stiff.

Edge Tape

This is a fusible or iron-on tape that is used in key places when constructing your jacket. It looks a bit like bias tape, as described below, but it is best suited for straight line application. It is used on the break or roll line of the jacket, the gorge and the front edge of a lapel, on the front or leading edge of the jacket and on the shoulder seams. It can also be used, carefully, round the armhole edge and the back neck, although a fusible bias tape is easier to apply and use in these areas. Edge tape helps give sharper and more structured finished edges to our jacket and helps the lapel, if there is one, to 'roll' and sit better.

Fusible Bias Tape

This is very similar to the edge tape, but it is cut on the bias and has a line of stitching through it. The stitched line on the tape is placed on the seam line of the garment and fused (ironed) into place. This tape is used round the back neck and the armholes to stabilize them before sewing.

Edgefix/Hem Band

Edgefix is a well-known brand of fusible hem band, although there are others on the market. It is about 4cm (1¼in) wide, with long perforations close to one edge. It is fused onto the hem of the jacket, sleeve hems, pocket tops, vents and plackets. The perforation is placed where the hem is to be folded up and it makes really sharp edges without having to press too heavily.

Shoulder Pads

These are so useful. Many of us do not like them, but they certainly make a difference to your jacket. They add structure to the shoulders and hold the jacket better. There are several types and weights of shoulder pads that can be purchased and self-made ones can work very well. Choose carefully, making sure that you select the

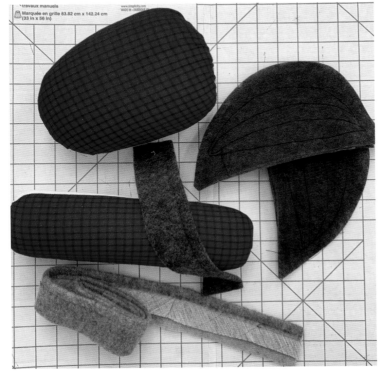

Shoulder pads, sleeve head and tailor's hams.

right shape for your jacket; that is, standard shoulder pads for set-in sleeves or raglan shoulder pads for raglan and dolman sleeves. And remember, a very light shoulder pad can make a big difference to the hang of your jacket.

Sleeve Head

This is something that many sewers will not have come across before. It is basically a narrow piece of wadding that is stitched onto the inside of the sleeve cap or the very top of the sleeve before it is stitched into the armhole. A sleeve head helps the sleeve sit much better on the shoulder after it is inserted, rounding the shoulder out slightly over the top of the arm and ensuring that the shoulder/armhole seam allowance does not show through to the sleeve when wearing the jacket. Sleeve heads can be purchased or made from lambswool wadding or other wadding that you might have available. It really does make a difference to the way the sleeve and shoulder sit when you are wearing your jacket.

Thread, Buttons and Trims

These are obvious requirements for any sewing project, but the main one is thread. It is always a good idea to buy your thread when you are buying your fabrics, to ensure that everything is to hand when you are ready to sew. Buttons can be bought later, especially if you are not sure what kind of buttons you want. However, you will need them in order to make buttonholes. Trims are more important if you are going to use them, because they are often stitched into the garment as you sew so you need to have them ready before you begin.

Pressing Equipment

This is really important for helping to get the best finish for your jacket. Whether you are using linen, silk, denim or tweed, pressing is the key to a really well-finished garment and it is even more critical with a tailored garment.

A good weight of iron makes pressing much easier and more successful. Do not be tempted by the very low-price bargain iron in the supermarket. It will probably be very lightweight and the temperature control may not be reliable.

In the same way, a good-sized, well-padded ironing board is a great investment for the sewing room. It makes pressing much easier and can double as a sewing table for pinning and preparing pieces for the sewing machine. A small sleeve board is also invaluable for pressing sleeve and trouser seams.

If you are a keen and regular sewer, then you may have a tailor's ham and sleeve roll. These are small, sawdust-filled, rounded pads that are used for pressing curves. The tailor's ham is a rounded cushion shape and the sleeve roll is sausage-shaped. They are quite solid and robust and are extremely useful for pressing the bust area, for shaping princess seams, for pressing sleeve seams and for pressing the jacket collar and lapels. They can be made or purchased and help make pressing much more successful.

Measurements

These are given in both metric and imperial. Work with one or the other as suits you; do not mix them as they do not always convert exactly.

Now you have everything ready to make your jacket and it is time to get started!

CUTTING AND PREPARING

As with all projects, be it sewing or decorating or making a cake, the time we take to prepare makes a significant difference to the end result. This is so true for sewing! We are often so keen to get started and then finish our next sewing project that we can end up rushing things and the end garment may not be just as perfect as it could be.

But now you are going to make a jacket and you will want it to look perfectly fitted and beautifully finished and therefore it is very important to take each stage of construction seriously and with no short cuts. So where do you start?

Preparing Your Fabric

Pre-shrink your fabric before you do anything. You can do this by washing it on a gentle wash in your machine. Dry it carefully and iron/press it to remove creases. Or you can steam press your fabric; use lots of steam and a press cloth to ensure there is no damage to your fabric. Whatever you choose, it is a very important first step. If you omit this step, then there is the possibility that as you are making your jacket it may shrink whilst you are pressing it during the construction process. Or worse, you have worn your jacket and had it cleaned, and it has shrunk. How disastrous would that be?

Preparing Your Pattern

Cut your paper pattern in the size that will fit you best. Remember that you can cut across size lines for smaller shoulders, wider waist, smaller hips, etc. If you can make adjustments to your paper pattern before you start cutting your fabric, then do so. Check body lengths and sleeve lengths and adjust the pattern if you are happy to do so. If you are not sure about making pattern adjustments before you cut any fabric, then cut your paper pattern as the size lines suggest and alterations can be made to your paper pattern after it has been fitted.

Making a Toile or Muslin

Make a practice jacket in calico or some other fabric that you may have available. If you can fit

Toile for fitting.

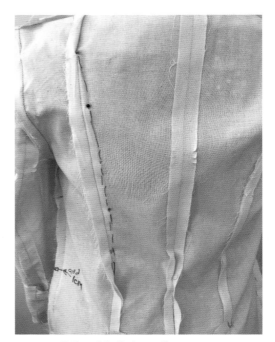

Toile with fitting adjustments.

your toile on yourself or your dress form (dress-maker's dummy) , that is excellent. If you need some help with fitting, you might want to try and find someone who can aid you. Transfer any adjustments you have made on your toile/muslin to your paper pattern after you have fitted your toile. These might include fuller/smaller bust adjustments, re-aligning of darts or princess seams, lengthening or shortening jacket body and/or sleeves, changes to the neckline and so on. Think about the fitting issues you have with a ready-to-wear jacket and try to eliminate those on your toile/muslin.

At this stage you can also make design changes if you wish. Perhaps you would like a centre back vent or you may prefer to remove a vent. You might want to add or remove a pocket. If you do make significant design changes, then it would be wise to practise the changes on calico before cutting your actual jacket fabric, just to ensure that the changes you have made look good, lie properly, are the right size and so on. Remember, the more preparation you do, the better the final result will be!

Cutting Your Fabric

Lay and pin your pattern on your fabric, making sure you have all the pieces that you will need to make your jacket. If you have a pattern, a check/plaid or a stripe to match, take care to fold your fabric so that the check/plaid will match on both sides of the folded fabric. Pinning the edges of the fabric together and laying your fabric on a smooth surface should help to keep it from dragging underneath and mis-aligning the check/plaid or print. If you do this, you will be much more confident that the fabric has not moved on the bottom fold before pin-ning and cutting your pattern pieces. If this proves too difficult it may be wise to open your fabric out and cut each piece singly, matching checks and patterns as you go. Taking care with this process will make your jacket look really special, so use the notches on the pattern pieces to match body pieces and sleeves to jacket.

Pattern Matching

Matching the pattern on your jacket pieces is not as difficult as it may seem if you follow a few simple steps. Firstly, find the notches on the side seams of your jacket pattern pieces. To match centre back and side back panels, place the notches of the jacket centre back and side back pieces on the same line of the check/plaid or print. Use a clear ruler or your French curve to make sure your notches are properly aligned, then pin your pattern pieces to your fabric. In the same way, the centre and side front panels can be matched by using the pattern notches. Finally, side seams can be matched, again by using notches. Another useful mark on the paper pattern is the waistline mark and this can also be used to match panels. Sleeves can be matched to armholes in the same way – by using notches on the front and back armhole edges and sleeve pieces.

Normal fabric cutting practice would dictate that all pattern pieces are laid out and pinned to the fabric before any cutting is started. This ensures that there is enough fabric and that all pieces of pattern can be properly laid out and accommodated. However, in order to pattern-match really accurately it will be necessary to cut some pieces of your jacket fabric before the

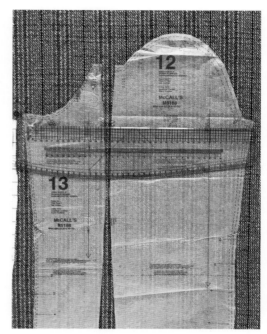

Using notches to pattern-match.

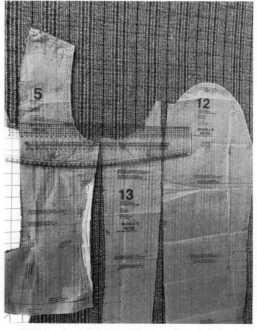

Side back piece cut and placed on fabric to pattern-match sleeves.

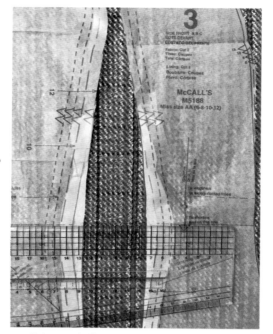

Using waistline marks to pattern-match.

rest of the fabric is cut, so that they can be matched against other pattern pieces still to be cut. It is doubly important therefore to ensure that you have enough fabric if you intend to pattern-match.

Remember that matching patterns, checks and stripes can only really be done on the seams. You will be able to match your stripes and checks on all seams and sleeve seams and where sleeves join the jacket body at the notches. But where the jacket shapes itself around your body, for example at bust, neckline and princess seams, the pattern pieces will not match. However, if you have cut your fabric carefully and have pattern-matched the seams, you should see a symmetry in the way the fabric is lying in the right and left fronts, the lapels and the sleeve seams.

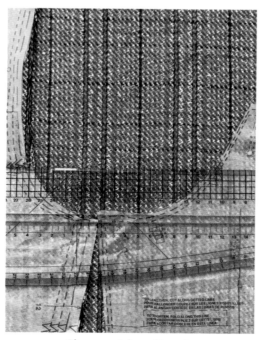

Sleeve notches aligned.

Checks aligned and matched.

Sleeves aligned and matched.

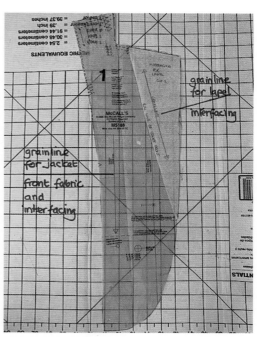

Pattern piece for lapel showing grainline for
lapel interfacing.

Cutting Your Interfacing

This is a very important step and the proper use
of interfacings will really help you to have a
good tailored finish to your jacket. You should
use a mediumweight interfacing for the jacket
front, the lapel, the undercollar and, if you have
them, side fronts. Use a lighter-weight fusible
for the back, side backs if you have them, the
front facing, the upper collar and, if you have
one, the neck facing. It is also a good idea to
fuse the upper part of the jacket sleeves with the
lighter-weight interfacing as it helps give the
sleeves a little more stability. For this, you
should cut the interfacing to fit the top of the
sleeve down to just above the elbow of the
sleeve and trim the lower edge with pinking
shears to ensure that you do not end up with an
interfacing line showing through your fabric
after it has been applied.

Then use the heavier of the two interfacings
for cutting a shoulder plate and back shoulder
reinforcement, doing this after you have begun
to stitch your jacket fronts and backs together.
This will be described more fully later in the
book.

When cutting the interfacing for the front of
your jacket, omit the lapel or rever. It should be
cut separately and you must use the roll line as
the straight grain guide for the interfacing on
the lapel. It is a good idea to make a 'pattern' of
the lapel and use that to cut your interfacing.

For the most accurate cutting out of your
interfacing, it is better to use your paper pattern
pieces. However, many people may prefer to
use the fabric pieces that are already cut out,
laying them on the interfacing and using them
as the pattern pieces. This will work if your fabric
has a bit of weight to it as it should not slip on
the interfacing and you will be able to cut round
it quite accurately. However, if your fabric is very

CHOICES FOR INTERFACING

Mediumweight interfacing
Jacket front, and side fronts if you have them
Lapel/rever
Undercollar
Back shoulder reinforcement
Front shoulder plate

Lighter-weight interfacing
Jacket back, and side backs if you have them
Front facing
Upper collar
Neck facing
Upper sleeve

Note: Cut the back shoulder reinforcement after you have stitched the jacket back pieces together and cut the front shoulder plates after you have stitched the jacket fronts together.

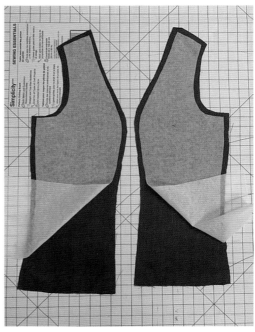

Interfacing cut and seam allowances removed before fusing.

lightweight, such as a light linen or a silk, then it is better to use your paper pattern pieces to cut your interfacings. If you do use your paper pattern to cut the interfacing, take care not to get all your newly cut fabric pieces confused when you take the paper pattern off them. Label them if necessary and once the interfacing is all cut out put all fabric and interfacing pieces back together with their own paper pattern piece.

Once you have cut all the interfacing pieces, the next step is to remove the seam allowances from all the mediumweight interfacing pieces; that is, the interfacing for the jacket front(s), lapel and undercollar. An effective way of doing this is to lay the interfacing pieces, glue side or rough side down, on your fabric pieces. This will stop the interfacing from slipping. Then carefully cut all round the edge of the interfacing pieces, being sure not to cut your fabric as well,

and removing the seam allowance so that you can eventually see your fabric piece underneath the interfacing. The reason the seam allowance is removed from the interfacing is to ensure that the jacket seams do not become too bulky or stiff after they have been stitched and pressed open. Do not cut away the hem allowances – only the seam allowances.

If you have darts in your jacket pattern, then you should remove the interfacing from the darts – before they are sewn. Again, this is to remove any potential bulk in the dart before it is pressed.

When you cut the interfacing for the lapel, only trim the seam allowance from the neck edge and the front edge. Do not trim along the roll line; there is no seam at the roll line and so there is no need to trim the interfacing there.

The lighter-weight interfacing does not require seam allowances to be trimmed as is

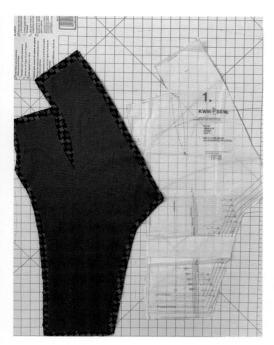

Darts cut out of interfacing before interfacing is fused.

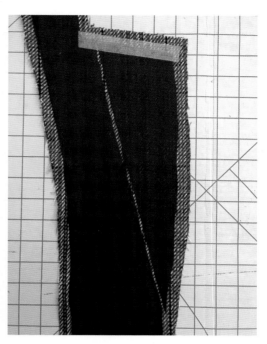

Interfacing on lapel with no seam allowance removed along roll line.

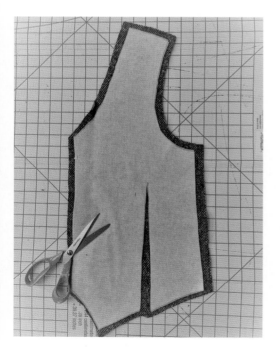

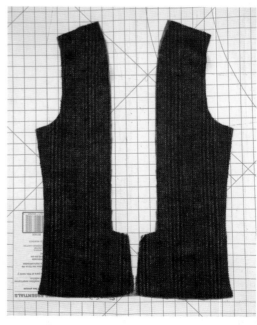

Interfacing on back of jacket with no seam allowances removed.

should not be heavy enough to make the seams bulky.

Cutting the Lining Fabric

It is a good idea to cut the lining fabric at this stage if you wish, being careful not to lose any pattern pieces. When you cut the lining remember to use all the pattern pieces necessary and also, very importantly, to add a pleat allowance to the centre back of the jacket lining if your pattern does not include one.

The easiest way to add a pleat to the lining of the jacket, if you do not have a separate pattern piece for the lining, is to place the jacket back pattern piece against the fold of the lining fabric and then slide it in from the fold by approximately 2.5cm (1in). When you cut the piece out, remember to cut across to the fold and not

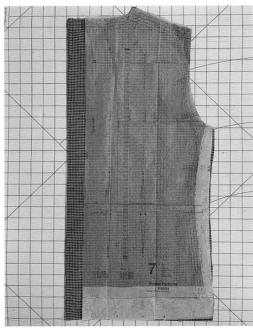

Pattern back piece on lining fabric with pleat added.

Pleat at centre back of lining.

along the centre back. In this way you will have added approximately 5cm (2in) to the centre back and this will make an excellent pleat.

If your jacket pattern has a centre back seam, you can still make a pleat in the same way. Lay your centre back pattern piece on the fold, with the seam allowance touching the fold of the lining fabric as closely as possible. Slide the pattern in from the fold as described above, then cut as if your pattern piece is on the fold of the fabric. Do not worry that the fold does not follow the same shape as the seam of your jacket. It is quite difficult to pleat a shaped seam and if you use the fold of the lining fabric, the resulting pleat will lie nicely inside your jacket.

This extra fabric in the centre back of the jacket allows the lining to move slightly and takes the strain out of the lining and jacket for longer-lasting wear. Again, if you have a patterned lining, pattern matching as described above would be impressive! But do not stress about it – it will be inside your jacket after all and the important thing is that the jacket fronts are lined identically.

KEEPING TRACK OF EVERYTHING

You will now have several pieces of fabric, interfacing and possibly your lining if you have cut it already. A good idea is to pin (one or two pins will be enough) each of your fabric, lining and interfacing pieces together with the appropriate paper pattern piece. This will help to prevent you from losing your fabric and interfacing pieces before you interface them and begin sewing. It will also help for easy identification of each piece of the jacket as you begin putting your jacket together.

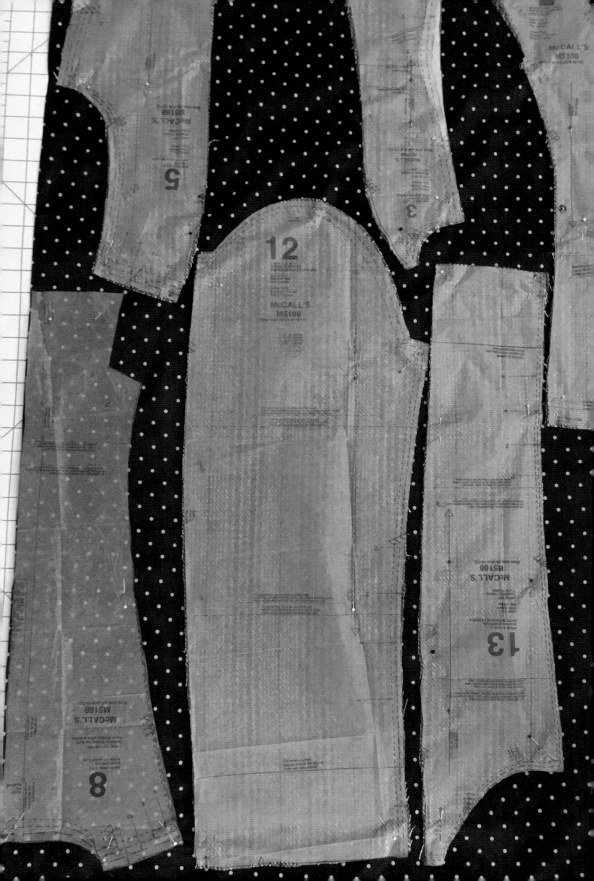

STARTING TO MAKE YOUR JACKET

So far, you have spent quite a lot of time getting everything ready and you will be desperate to start sewing. But we're not quite ready for the sewing machine just yet. The first part of the construction process is to fuse (by ironing on) all your interfacings and tapes. Be prepared for this to take some time.

Jacket side fronts laid as pair before fusing interfacing.

Applying Your Interfacings

For this you will need a good hot iron and a good press cloth. Plain ivory-coloured, silk organza makes an excellent press cloth, as it can withstand lots of heat and you can see through it. Make sure, however, if you do use silk organza as a press cloth, that it does not have any fancy threads running through it; these could melt and ruin your fabric and your inter-facing.

When you apply interfacing, what happens is that the heat of the iron melts the glue on the back of the interfacing and it sticks to the fabric. So the first thing to do is to make sure that you have the right side or the 'gluey' side of the interfacing against the wrong side of the fabric. It is usually a bit shiny in appearance and feels rougher than the non-gluey side. If you get this

Silk organza press cloth.

wrong, it could ruin your fabric pieces or your press cloth! If you're not sure which is the gluey side of the interfacing, test some small pieces on fabric scraps before you begin.

When you begin to apply the interfacing with the iron, it is very important not to 'iron' the interfacing onto your fabric but, instead, to hold the iron in place without moving it, for up to ten seconds at a time. Move the iron systematically over your garment pieces, holding it for up to ten seconds each time. This will ensure that there is enough time and heat to melt the glue and make the interfacing adhere. Do this until you have interfaced each piece entirely. If your interfacing bubbles at all, it has not been given enough time and heat with the iron.

Another important point to note is that if you drag the iron across the interfacing and fabric, the interfacing will very probably move and distort, so lift and lay the iron carefully whilst fusing your interfacing.

Note: Many interfacing instructions say to use a water spray when fusing your interfacing to your fabric. If you choose to use a water spray, remember that the iron has to evaporate the water before it can melt the glue so the process may take a little longer. In most cases a water spray is not necessary. Always test first, however, and find the method that suits your fabric best.

Make sure when you are applying your interfacing that you fuse to the wrong side of the fabric. If your fabric is such that it is hard to tell the right side from the wrong side, once you have decided which side you would prefer to be the right side, mark the wrong side of the fabric with chalk or removable tape. When you are ready to apply your interfacing, take matching pieces, for example the jacket fronts, and lay them both out (either on your ironing board or your table) wrong side up so that you've got a right and a left piece facing you. Remove the tape or brush the chalk mark away, then lay the interfacings glue side down on each piece

before you use the iron. In this way, you should end up with the interfacing applied to the correct side of the fabric and not end up with two left or two right panels.

Edge Tape and Bias Tape

These were mentioned in Chapter 1, but what are they? Edge tape and bias tape are usually about 1.5–2cm (approximately $5/8$ in) wide and both tapes are fusible; in other words they can be ironed on. The edge tape is a straight tape that is used along the straight edges of the jacket and the bias tape is, as it says, cut on the bias and is used round the armhole and the neck of the jacket. These tapes are used to give strength and stability to the seams in these particular areas of the garment.

The edge tape is fused to the leading or front edge of the jacket, along the inside or jacket side of the roll line and up towards and then across the front shoulder. The bias tape is fused right round the armhole and round the back neckline of the jacket.

It is important to apply all the interfacing pieces first, before you apply your tapes. You then apply the necessary tapes to your jacket pieces, placing them over the seam line, so that when you sew your jacket together you will be stitching along or through the centre of the tapes. This will ensure good strong seams and will prevent any stretching. The tape edges can go right to the cut edge of your fabric piece and do not have to be trimmed.

Take your time applying the tapes to ensure that they are in the right place and are well fused or stuck to the jacket pieces. Remember that in some cases the shoulder tapes and the armhole tapes have to be applied after the fronts and maybe the backs of the jacket have been stitched together. For example, if your jacket has princess seams running up through

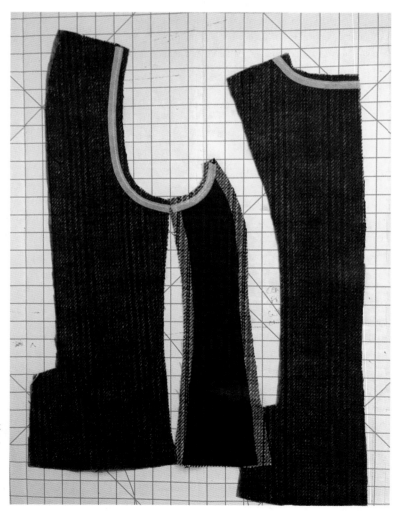

Bias tape applied to neck and armhole.

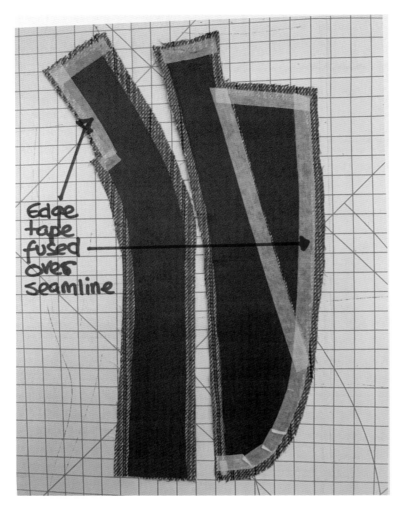

Edge
tape
fused
over
seamline

Edge tape on straight
edges and over seamlines.

to the shoulders then the jacket front pieces will need to be stitched together and seams pressed open before the shoulder tapes are applied. Likewise, if the princess seams run into the armhole, then stitch the centre front and side fronts together, press the seams open and then apply the armhole tape. The same rule is used for princess seams on the back of the jacket. Do not worry if you have applied your shoulder tapes before stitching your seams together. It will not cause a problem, but it is better practice to apply the tapes after the seams have been stitched.

Note: The armhole tape should be applied in two pieces, front and back. The side seam of the jacket does not need to be stitched before the armhole tape is applied.

Edgefix

Edgefix is the straight tape we put on hems, vents and pocket tops. If you are making patch pockets, it may be a good idea to apply Edgefix

Edge tape still to be fused over shoulder seams after princess seams stitched.

along the top fold of the pocket at this point. Place the long perforations exactly on the fold-line at the top of the pocket with the remainder of the tape running to the top edge of the pocket. This will mean that the fold at the top of the pocket is all interfaced with Edgefix. The result will be a nice sharp fold or turnover at the top of the patch pocket.

For the hems, sleeve hems and any vents, Edgefix tape will be applied later in the construction process.

At long last you are nearly ready to start stitching your jacket together! The last thing to do before you start, if you have not already done so, is to make sure that you test your sewing machine with your chosen fabrics and thread. Check tensions and stitch length. Practise buttonholes, pocket finishes and any other sewing technique that you want to be perfect before you actually begin sewing your jacket.

SEWING THE JACKET'S OUTER SHELL

At last you can begin to sew your jacket together. The preparation will have taken quite some time and can be frustrating. Most of us love to sit at the machine, press the foot pedal and stitch! Jacket making teaches patience and time management. Without the preparation, your jacket will not have the tailored finish that you are striving for and you will not be as happy with it as you could be if you take the time to prepare your fabric in the correct way.

Sewing the jacket is almost the easiest and quickest part of making the jacket. As ever with making a garment, the preparation and the finishing are the parts of construction that take the most time. So enjoy your time at the sewing machine.

Sewing Sequence

When we stitch any garment, there is normally a clear order or construction process in how we put it together. For a dress, we start by sewing darts, making the dress front, then the back, then we join at the shoulder and side seams, sew in the zip and finish the hems. All garments have a construction order and jackets are no dif-ferent. We start with darts and pockets and then move to seams, fronts and backs, then the collar and we end with sleeves and hems.

Darts

The first thing to do is to stitch any darts that you have on your jacket. Stitch and press them according to your pattern instructions. If you feel that your fabric is too heavy to press your dart in the normal way, you can slash the centre fold of the dart after you have stitched it and then press the dart open on the inside of the jacket. In this way it will be less bulky and less likely to show through onto the right side of your jacket. If your chosen fabric is quite light and, after pressing, shows through on the right side of the fabric, then use a piece of paper or light card. Place the paper or card between the wrong side of the fabric and the stitched dart, butting the paper or card along the stitched line of the dart, so that the card is between the dart and the fabric, then press in the normal way. This should prevent the fold of the dart from showing through on the right side of your jacket.

SEWING A CLEAN DART

Starting at the wide end of the dart, gently curve your machine stitching towards the fold of the dart and finish the last centimetre or half inch by stitching along the foldline of the dart to the finishing point. Chain off your stitches as this will lock the stitching and prevent the need for backstitching, which can be messy at the end of a dart. To chain off your stitches, keep stitching for about 5cm (2in) after you have reached the end of the dart, even though there is no fabric beneath the presser foot. This will leave a short 'tail' of thread that should not be cut off and which will effectively tie off the stitches at the end of the dart.

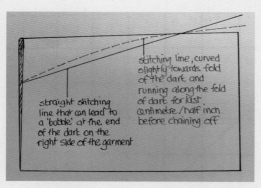

Stitching dart with curve for smoother finish.

Pockets

Now is the time to make your pockets if you have them on your jacket. There are two types of pockets that you can make: patch pockets, which will be stitched onto the front of your jacket, or internal pockets, which lie inside the jacket and are finished by stitching a bound edge or a welt. The latter are sometimes called jetted pockets.

If your pocket crosses a princess seam down

the front of your jacket, this will need to be stitched and pressed open before the pocket can be applied. Likewise, if your pocket lies over a dart, it should be stitched and pressed before the pocket is stitched.

Making an Unlined Patch Pocket

To make an unlined patch pocket, it is a good idea to make a cardboard template of the finished size of the pocket. Lay this template inside the pocket fabric piece and press your seam allowances inwards over the template. Start by pressing down the fold at the top of the pocket then press the seam allowances in. You may want to trim back the seam allowance at this point to about 5mm (¼in), leaving the turnover at the top of the pocket at its full size. If you wish, you can tack (baste) the seam allowances down to hold them in place, before you carefully align the pocket on the jacket front and topstitch in place. If you do tack the seam allowances first, try to tack in and away from the stitch line as this will make it much easier to remove the tacking after the pocket has been stitched in place. Also check that tacking will

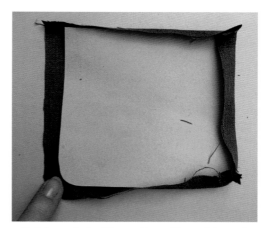

Patch pocket with cardboard template and seam allowances being pressed and trimmed.

not leave a mark after it has been removed.

Making a Lined Patch Pocket

If you are lining your patch pocket, cut your lining the same size as the pocket then remove the turnover fold at the top of the pocket from the lining. This will ensure that the lining does not

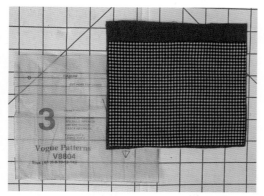

Pocket and lining fabric cut with lining seam allowance very slightly trimmed back.

come to the very top of the inside of the pocket. Once you have trimmed the fold from the lining, trim the seam allowance of the lining by 2–3mm (1/8 in) round the remaining three sides.

Stitch the top edges of the pocket fabric and lining, right sides together, leaving about 5cm (2in) open in the centre of the seam, and press the seam towards the lining.

Turn the lining right side to right side with the pocket piece and, matching the edges exactly, stitch the pocket and the lining together. Because the lining is slightly smaller than the pocket, when the pocket is turned through, the seam joining the lining to the pocket fabric will be 2–3mm (1/8in) in from the folded edge and will turn in slightly and therefore will not show when the pocket is stitched to your jacket. Check your seam allowances and trim if necessary. Turn the pocket through the gap left in the top seam and ease it out. Close the top seam with a small slip stitch. Press carefully. Finally, place the pocket on your jacket front and top-stitch in place.

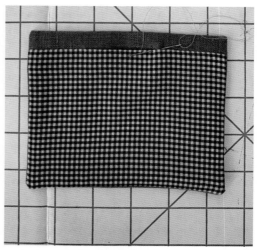

Pocket stitched and lining closed with slip stitch.

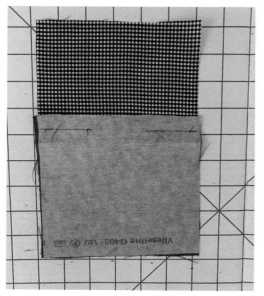

Pocket and lining stitched together with opening in middle of seam..

Welt Pockets

Sewing your welt or jetted pockets can be a daunting prospect but, taken one step at a time, they will become easier to understand and will look fantastic when you have completed them. If your pattern has welt pockets included, then you should have all the pattern pieces you require to make your pockets and full instructions about how to make them. If you are adding welt pockets, then you will have to cut the welts and the pocket bag from your fabric and lining. A double welt pocket has two welt strips and a single welt pocket has one welt strip.

The first thing to do is to mark the pocket on the right side of your jacket front. If your pattern has welt pockets included, these marks will have been transferred to the jacket pieces after the interfacing was fused and before any seams or darts were stitched. Check your pattern pieces to make sure the pockets are in the right place and correctly marked. If you are adding welt pockets, decide where exactly you want them to be and mark carefully. Remember to mark both jacket fronts accurately if adding pockets at both sides. Lopsided pockets will not look good!

Now take a rectangular piece of interfacing that is 3cm (1¼in) longer than your pocket opening and about 6cm (2¼in) deep and fuse this to the wrong side of the pocket opening. This will give stability to the pocket opening.

Take your welt strips (usually about 7.5cm (3in) wide and 2cm (¾in) longer than the pocket opening) and cut pieces of lightweight interfacing the same size, one for each welt strip. Fuse all the welt strips on the wrong side. Then fold the welt strips in half lengthways, wrong sides together, and stitch.

Place each strip along the pocket mark you made earlier, with the raw edges butted together and lying along the pocket mark. The folded edges will be away from the pocket

Pocket marked on right side of fabric with welt strips cut and ready to sew.

Welts stitched in place.

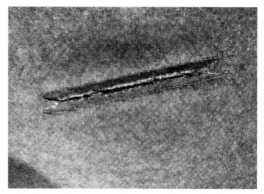

Pocket cut open, with triangular cuts at each end (viewed from wrong side).

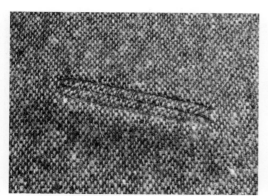

Welt strips turned through to wrong side, pressed lightly and tacked in place.

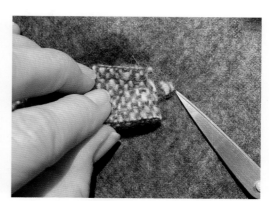

Triangle to be stitched down to pocket welts.

mark. Make sure the welts are centred – remember they are longer than the pocket opening. Pin and tack to hold them in place. Mark the ends of the pocket opening onto the welts, then stitch with the machine along the centre of each welt from end mark to end mark. Remember to sew only to the end mark and not to the end of the welt. Finish the end of each stitching line securely by backstitching with the machine for a short distance.

If you are happy that the pocket welts are stitched straight and are positioned properly, then the pockets can be cut open. Use small sharp scissors and cut from the centre of the pocket mark out towards each end, but not to the actual end of the pocket mark. You should stop at least 1cm (^{1}/2 in) before the end mark and then cut out to the end of each stitching line, making a triangle.

The longer the triangle at each end of the cutting line, the easier it is to manage the next steps. Turn the welts through to the wrong side of the jacket front and check that they are lying flat. If they are slightly puckered at any of the corners, it is because you have not cut quite far enough to the end of the stitching line, so turn back and snip again if necessary. You actually have to cut very close to the stitching line so beware not to snip too far. Small snips with the

scissors are safer. Once you are happy with the welts and how they are lying, press them lightly in place and tack them shut on the right side of the jacket. These tacking stitches will be removed later.

Now the welts must be fixed in place on the wrong side of the jacket. To do this, go to the wrong side of the jacket front. Take the ends of the welts and gently pull to ensure they are lying flat and, at the same time, pull the triangles out too. This will help the welts to lie flat on the right side of the jacket. Then, looking at the triangles, isolate them and the welts from your jacket front and stitch the triangles to the welts along each end of the pocket opening. It is a

Pocket bag pinned ready for stitching to welt strip.

good idea to reinforce your stitching here to ensure that your pocket does not come apart with use.

Turn again to the right side and check that the pocket opening looks perfect. If you wish at this stage, you may want to topstitch all round the edge of the pocket opening. Use a straight stitch and stitch in the ditch. This is not necessary but it may help to secure the pocket opening better if using a heavy fabric.

Now the pocket bag must be attached. This can be cut in either one or two pieces. Your pattern may have pocket lining pieces included so use these. Otherwise, the easiest option is to cut one piece of lining for the pocket bag. The lining should be cut 2cm (¾in) wider than the pocket opening and twice the required pocket depth plus 3cm (1¼in).

Take the bottom edge of the pocket lining piece and pin it to the bottom welt on the inside of the jacket. Stitch together on the seam allowance and beside the existing stitching. Then fold the pocket lining over and attach the top end to the top welt. Stitch to the top welt, as before, and secure at each end. All that is now left to do is to stitch the sides of the pocket bag. Isolate the pocket bag from the jacket and stitch both sides of the pocket bag securely. Turn to the right side of the jacket and remove the tacking stitches from the welts.

You have now made a beautiful welt pocket!

Completed welt pocket.

Seams

You have constructed some of the most challenging visible parts of your jacket and at last it is now time to begin to put the jacket pieces together.

You may have already stitched the front (princess) seams of your jacket together in order to sew your pockets, so now you can move on to the seams for the rest of the body of the jacket. The usual order for putting a garment together is to make the front(s), then make the back, then join the fronts and back together at the sides and the shoulders. So it is with a jacket. Stitch the back of your jacket together, starting with the centre back seam if you have one, and moving to the side back seams if you have them.

Back Vents

Your jacket may have one or two vents on the hem edge of the back seam(s). Now is the time to make these. If you have one vent on the back of your jacket, it will be placed on the centre back seam of the jacket. If you have two vents on the back of your jacket, then you will probably have a centre back seam and definitely have two side back seams. The vents will be placed on the side back seams. At this stage of construction, making the vents is a simple process. Later in the book there is a full description of how to mitre vents for a professional finish.

When tacking (basting) the tops of the vents in place, for a two-vent jacket, press your side back seams towards the centre of your jacket before tacking; this ensures that the vents, when seen from the outside or right side of the jacket, will be folded out from the centre towards the side seams. If you are sewing with a bulky or tweed fabric, the seams should be pressed open and the seam allowance just above the vent snipped in order to press the

MAKING A MITRE ON A VENT

1. Press in seam allowances and hem allowance on item to be mitred.

2. Open out hem allowance and mark on the bottom of the hem the point where the seam allowances (still folded in) meet the hem.

Seam allowances folded in and marked on hem with snip or pins.

3. Open out seam allowances and fold hem allowance back up. Mark on seam edges the point where the hem allowance meets the seams.

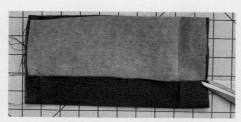

Hem allowance folded up and marked on side seams with snip or pins.

4. Place a pin exactly at the point where hem and seam allowance folds intersect.

Pins placed where fold of hem and seam meets.

Mitre folded and ready to machine-stitch.

5. Fold right sides together, matching the side and hem pins/marks. Do not be concerned if the fabric seems lopsided when right sides are folded together.

6. Stitch securely from the side and hem pins/marks direct to the centre pin.

Stitching line from fold intersection to hem and seam edges.

7. Trim seam allowance and turn through. Press.

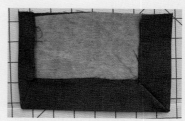

Finished mitres.

Mitred vent on jacket back before lining attached.

Jacket with vents pressed towards centre back seam and back seams pressed open.

fully the first time. The instructions and photographs here explain how to sew a successful mitred vent, where both seam and hem allowances are the same and also where the seam allowance is narrower than the hem allowance. Use these instructions to mitre the vents on your jacket hem and sleeves.

Undercollar

The undercollar is the next piece to be stitched to the jacket. This can be a confusing piece of the garment, so read your pattern piece carefully and make sure all your notches and pattern markings are correct. This will help to ensure that the undercollar is attached the right way up. The undercollar is usually cut in two pieces and stitched together with a centre back seam. Also, the undercollar is always cut on the bias; this ensures that it can roll over smoothly when the jacket is finished.

The centre seam of the undercollar pieces should be stitched and pressed open. It is important to ensure that the correct edge of the

vent to one side.

For a single-vent jacket, the vent should be pressed to the left on the inside before tacking, so that it is facing the right direction on the outside of the jacket. A single vent on a lady's jacket should fold right over left when looking at it from the outside or right side of the jacket. On a gentleman's jacket the single vent runs left over right. Press the centre back seam open and, again, snip the seam allowance just above the vent, in order to press the vent to one side.

Once the back of the jacket is stitched and all seams are pressed open, stitch the fronts and back together at the side seams and press those seams open. Finally, stitch the shoulder seams and press them open too. You now have the beginnings of your jacket. Check the fit at this stage and make any adjustments that you may require.

The best and most professional finish for vents is a mitred finish and this can often be a bit confusing to understand and stitch success-

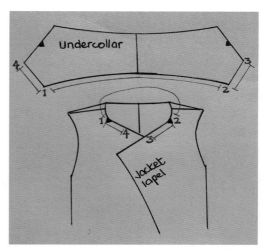

Diagram of undercollar and jacket neckline.

undercollar is stitched to the neckline of the jacket so take care to follow all notches and markings. Sometimes it is quite difficult to decide which is the longer, outside edge and which is the neck edge of the undercollar (and the corresponding collar piece) but usually the shorter edge of the collar piece is the neck edge that will be attached to the jacket.

The diagram here shows how the undercollar should be attached to the jacket. The easiest way to do this is to break the stitching into steps and to sew the collar on in three separate stages. The shortest edge of the collar, the neck edge, attaches around the neck of the jacket and onto the lapel. In the diagram this is shown as points 1 to 2.

There should be a notch on the paper pattern piece across the top of the lapel or rever and this notch should have been transferred to the fabric pieces. This notch marks the point where the first line of stitching (that is, the neck edge of the undercollar) should start and finish (points 1 to 2 in the diagram). A good idea is to place a pin at the exact point where your stitching

must start or end. This gives the eye a focus for where to finish when sewing your undercollar and jacket seam. It also shows you where you have to pivot when finishing sewing the under-collar onto the jacket.

When stitching from point 1 to point 2, finish stitching 1.5cm (5/8 in) from each end of the undercollar piece. If you stitch to the very edge of the undercollar, it will not be possible to pivot the collar to sew the next part of the collar to the lapel.

Next, the short straight side of the undercol-lar must be stitched to the lapel. This looks quite difficult as you appear to have to sew a sharp corner. To do this, snip into the seam allowance on the jacket only, being careful not to snip too far. This will allow you to 'open' out the jacket lapel to stitch the straight sides of the undercol-lar to the lapel (points 2 to 3 and 1 to 4 on the diagram). It is important at this point to gently ease out the lapel when you are sewing from 2 to 3 and 1 to 4 so that you do not get a crease or bubble in the corner of the collar where it is attached.

Collar with pins in before stitching.

Jacket with collar half-stitched and snip made into seam before pivoting.

Jacket collar seam allowance snipped before side of collar is stitched to jacket.

Jacket with undercollar stitched and no puckers.

Jacket with collar seam snipped and pressed open.

Jacket with undercollar successfully stitched.

Once you are happy with the finished result, snip the collar and neck seam at regular intervals to allow it to open out, then gently press the whole seam open. Using a sleeve roll or tailor's ham may help with pressing this seam open, as it is a shaped seam and will not press easily on the ironing board. Press the seam open in stages using different parts of the tailor's ham to suit the curve of the seam. Remember to use a press cloth.

Sleeves

Now we come to the sleeves. Most good jacket patterns have a two-piece sleeve; the reason for this is that the overall sleeve shape is much better and more natural than with a one-piece sleeve. If you look at a ready-to-wear jacket you will see that the sleeve hangs in a slight curve towards the front of the garment. Standing in front of a mirror, it is easy to see that our arms naturally rest in a very similar position, so a two-piece sleeve gives the best and most natural result and a more comfortable sleeve. It is possible to find three-piece sleeves on some patterns but they are not so common.

Sleeves Without Vents

If your jacket has two-piece sleeves and no vent at the cuff, the upper sleeve must be stitched to the lower sleeve piece along the long edge of both sleeve pieces, matching notches and starting from the sleeve hem, stitching up to the armhole. Sewing in this direction will ensure that the sleeve pieces do not slip or move during sewing and the hem of the sleeve is not mismatched. It may be that there is some ease

included in this seam and this should be incorporated in the top half of the seam, towards the armhole. The ease allows for slightly more shape and fabric in the upper sleeve. The seam just stitched is called the hindseam. Press the hindseam open.

Now is a good time to check the length of the sleeve. If a toile or muslin has been made, all necessary alterations to the sleeve, including length, will have been marked on the toile and transferred to the paper pattern. This means that the sleeve length should be correct when the sleeve pieces are cut from the jacket fabric. If you are not sure, tack the remaining sleeve seam and fit the sleeve for length at this point. You may have to tack the sleeve into your jacket to do this more accurately. Make any necessary alterations or adjustments at this point, unpicking the tacking stitches to open the sleeve out again.

Edgefix tape is now applied to the hem of the

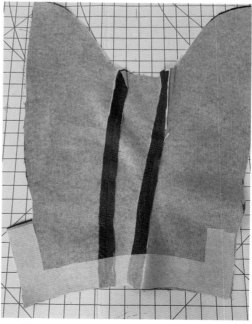

Sleeves with vent and interfacing fused before hemming.

sleeve. As described in Chapter 1, Edgefix is a fusible tape approximately 4cm (1½in) wide, with a line of long perforations close to one edge. The tape is applied so that the line of perforations is placed exactly where the hem fold-line will be once the hem is turned up, with the wider part of the tape in the hem itself. The tape is fused into place with a dry iron and a press cloth. The tape gives the hem of the sleeves and the jacket more structure and a sharper, crisper finish.

Place the tape carefully on the hem of the sleeve, making sure that the perforations are exactly where the hem should be folded up. Fuse the tape to the sleeve hem, crossing the hindseam if the jacket sleeve has no vent. If the sleeve has a vent, then a piece of interfacing should be cut and fused to the bottom edge of the sleeve as shown in the photograph here.

If your jacket sleeves do not have vents, stitch the remaining sleeve seam and press.

Sleeve Vents

Sleeve vents may be included on your sleeve pattern; if they are, it is necessary to make them before the sleeve is fully constructed. It is much easier to stitch a vent or a cuff detail on a flat piece of fabric than stitching it into a sleeve already made. The vent will be at the bottom of the hindseam, so this seam is left open and the sleeve pieces are stitched together along the shorter seam. Instead of using Edgefix tape at the sleeve hem, as described above, this time a piece of interfacing is cut and fused to the bottom of the sleeve, as shown in the photograph.

Making sleeve vents is fully described in Chapter 7. Once the sleeve vents are completed, the remaining sleeve seam can be stitched ready for the next stage.

Sleeve Head

Sleeve head is the next thing to be applied to the sleeve. This is a form of wadding that is stitched round the top of the sleeve (the area also known as the sleeve cap). It is approximately 20cm (8in) long at the most and about 2.5cm (1in) wide. It is stitched round the sleeve cap before the sleeve is inserted into the jacket. Sleeve head gives structure to the top of the sleeve where it meets the shoulder and supports the jacket better across the shoulders (along with shoulder pads, which will be explained and described later in this chapter). The final result should look smooth and slightly rounded and should hang beautifully.

Sleeve head can be purchased from a good sewing retailer or tailoring supplier. Alternatively, wadding or lambswool can be cut into strips and used as sleeve head. Such wadding should be cut on the bias, as should any light-weight casing for the lambswool. It is important that the weight of the sleeve head is appropriate for the fabric being used to make the jacket. If the jacket is being made from tweed, a slightly heavier sleeve head will work best. For a light-weight summer linen jacket, a lighter sleeve head will give a better result.

The sleeve head strips are centred on the inside of the sleeve cap and the outer edge of the sleeve head should be placed at the raw edge of the sleeve cap. The sleeve head should be stitched to the sleeve cap just within the seam allowance. This means that when the sleeve is being attached to the jacket body, the stitching will go through the sleeve head again. It will then be hidden by the jacket lining when that is attached. If commercial sleeve head is used, it will be much too deep and should be trimmed back to about 2.5cm (1in). The sleeve head should not interfere with the shoulder and the shoulder pad when it is fitted.

Once the sleeve head is stitched to each sleeve, it is time to insert the sleeves. On a traditionally

Purchased sleeve head pinned to sleeve cap before stitching.

6 | 7 | 8 | 9 | 10 | 11 | 12 | 13 |

Sleeve head stitched and trimmed back.

constructed or tailored garment, whether it be a jacket, dress or blouse, sleeves almost always have to be eased into the armhole because there is usually a little too much sleeve for the armhole. This is known as sleeve ease, which means there is a little extra fabric at the head of the sleeve, making the fit better over the top half of the arm and ensuring that the sleeve does not feel too tight on the upper arm. There are many arguments for and against having sleeve ease, but it usually improves the fit at the top of the sleeve and gives better mobility of the sleeve when wearing the jacket.

Only the top part of the sleeve cap needs to be eased. A good rule is to use the notches on the sleeve pattern and ease from the front sleeve notch up and round to the back sleeve notches. Many patterns give a much shorter area for easing across the sleeve cap but this can result in gathering at the top of the sleeve, especially if there is quite a lot of ease in the sleeve pattern. In this case, increase the area to be eased and use the notches, as mentioned above, as the start and stop point for easing. Note that there is never any easing done on the underarm part of the sleeve.

A confident sewer will be able to pin a sleeve into the armhole and ease with pins only before sewing. An alternative is to sew two rows of long tacking stitch with the machine, tying off the beginning of each row and leaving a long thread at the finishing end of each row. Make sure that both rows start and finish at the same point and that they are approximately 5mm (¼in) apart and within the seam allowance. Once stitched, hold the long threads on either the inside or the outside of the sleeve and gently pull the fabric back until it begins to gather slightly. Do not worry if you gather the sleeve cap too much, as this can be pulled back as required when pinning the sleeve before stitching. This method allows the sleeve ease to be equally spread around the top of the jacket armhole.

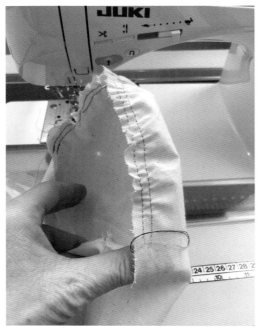

Sleeve ease demonstrated on calico.

Start to pin your sleeve into the jacket from the front and back arm notches then pin down round the underarm. Ensure that the underarm of the sleeve lies flat and without any gathering or puckering. Gradually pin up round the sleeve to the sleeve cap, pinning both sides evenly until the whole sleeve is pinned and ready to sew. In this way, the ease can be balanced properly across the whole of the sleeve cap without causing any unwanted gathering or puckering in one small part of the sleeve.

When sewing the sleeve in, sew from the inside of the sleeve. It is much easier to sew 'inside the circle' than to try and sew 'outside the circle'. The machining will be more accurate as the sleeve can be seen the whole time. It is also much easier to manipulate the garment whilst sewing the sleeve in if sewing from the inside. It may be tempting to use the free-arm facility on your sewing machine, but there is more risk that the sleeve will sew with puckers on the seam and will need to be unpicked and

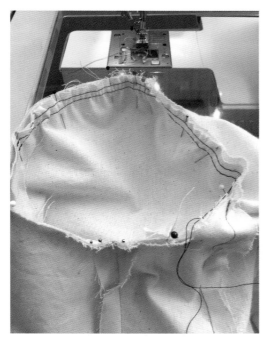

Sleeve pinned and eased around sleeve cap with no easing at underarm.

Sleeve being stitched from inside.

stitched again as it is not possible to see the sleeve whilst stitching this way.

If the sleeves have been correctly stitched into the jacket, they should curve slightly forward of the jacket body when on a dress form or clothes hanger. Try the jacket on at this point and decide if it feels comfortable or not. Make any necessary adjustments if required, then gently press the sleeve seam from just below the sleeve cap and down to the notches on either side, but do not press the underarm part of the seam. This should never be pressed. Press the seam away from the jacket and into the sleeve. Take care not to press the seam near the sleeve head either as this will crush the top of the sleeve. Press gently.

Shoulder Pads

Shoulder pads make a significant difference to the hang and tailored look of a jacket so they are fitted at this point, before moving on to the next stage of construction. Many of us do not like the idea of shoulder pads, feeling that they might accentuate the shoulders too much. However, the right weight of shoulder pads will support the shoulders of the jacket when it is being worn and will improve the overall hang and fit of the jacket across the shoulders. Shoulder pads come in various weights and sizes, and they are also available for raglan sleeves. The shoulder pads used in a tailored jacket are standard-shaped shoulder pads and are the last thing fitted to the jacket before the lining goes in.

There are various types of shoulder pads on the market. If pads are purchased from a tailoring supplier, they will probably be put together in layers. These layers can be separated and layers removed or added if necessary before being loosely stitched together again. If pads are bought from the local haberdashery, they will probably be made from covered foam. It is not possible to reduce the overall weight of foam pads. Therefore if you are using foam pads, as in the photograph here, make sure they are not

Shoulder pads with layers removed.

Jacket with foam shoulder pads.

too heavy and stiff for your jacket.

It is best to position shoulder pads either whilst wearing the jacket or by putting it on a dress form. The pad needs to be positioned slightly forward of the shoulder towards the front of the jacket; this helps to fill out the hollow just below the shoulder and above the bust/chest. Fix the straight edge of the shoulder pad so that it meets the edge of the sleeve cap seam. In other words, the shoulder pad sits out into the sleeve and supports the sleeve cap. Pin the shoulder pad in place and loosely stitch it to the shoulder seam allowance. Then, carefully smoothing the shoulder pad down, catch the bottom corners of the pad to the armhole seam with a loose stitch. Alternatively, fit and pin the shoulder pad in place along the shoulder seam and stitch it by hand, quite loosely, round the armhole seam. Catch the curved side to the shoulder seam with a bar tack. This method is slightly trickier to hand-sew but just as effective. Either way, it is important not to fix the shoulder pad too tightly or it may cause the jacket to pucker on the outside. If the shoulder pad is constructed in layers, it is not necessary to stitch through all the layers.

Layered shoulder pad pinned in place slightly forward of shoulder seam.

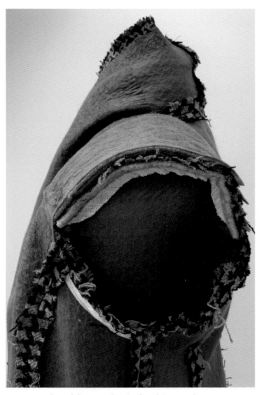

Shoulder pad stitched into place.

Jacket Hem

In order to achieve a good crisp hem, Edgefix is now fused along the hem of the jacket, in the same way as it was used in the sleeves. The tape is placed so that the long perforations lie on the hem foldline when the hem is turned up. The tape is fused into place with a dry iron and a press cloth.

The outside of your jacket is now almost completed; it is now time to make the lining.

Jacket hem with Edgefix applied.

Jacket ready for lining.

SEWING THE JACKET LINING

You are now getting to the final stages of making your jacket and this is where you can experiment with your creative side by choosing a wonderful lining. It is quite popular to use a contrasting or patterned lining inside a garment and it gives a secret dimension of pleasure when wearing an elegant jacket or coat that has a lovely surprise inside.

Of course, there are practical reasons for lining your jacket. The first reason for using a lining is that it hides all the work on the inside of the jacket; it removes the need for finishing seam allowances and hides the interfacings. Another reason is that it makes the jacket much easier to slip on and off over other garments so long as a cotton lining has not been used. Finally, the lining takes the strain of wear away from the outer fabric, increasing its lifetime and preventing the jacket fabric from stretching out of shape with wear.

Lining fabric should therefore be chosen carefully. It must be an appropriate weight for the jacket. If it is too flimsy it may wear at the seams quite quickly. If it is too heavy then the jacket may feel cumbersome, too warm or bulky to wear comfortably and the lining may affect the hang of the finished jacket. The lining fabric should always be lighter in weight than the jacket fabric.

Remember also that your lining fabric need not necessarily come from the selection of lining fabrics in your chosen fabric store. You can use any fabric you like if you think it will work with your jacket. Many blouse and dress fabrics are light and soft enough to be used as lining fabric. Choose carefully and you will wear your jacket comfortably with joy and pride.

Making Your Jacket Lining

You will use nearly all your jacket pattern pieces to cut out your lining fabric. However, you will not cut the jacket front facing in lining fabric because you have already cut that in jacket fabric. Some patterns will have specific lining pattern pieces included to use for the lining but most will use the jacket pieces. Check on each pattern piece as there should be instructions detailing what to cut in fabric, lining and interfacing on each pattern piece.

Alternatively, if you are lining a jacket that is not specifically meant to be lined, then you will cut all pattern pieces except the front facing and the collar pieces in lining fabric.

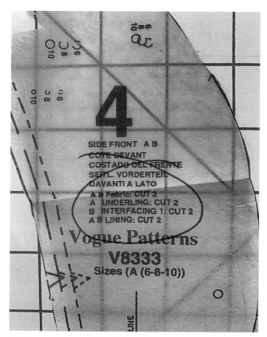

Pattern piece detailing what to cut in fabric, lining and interfacing.

The reason for adding a fold or pleat to the centre back lining is that it allows the lining to give a little during wear and not to strain against the jacket. It allows the lining to move slightly when the jacket is being worn and this takes the strain away from the lining seams as well as supporting the jacket itself.

Once all the lining pieces have been cut out, notched and marked, start stitching the back of the lining first. Make the pleat by folding the centre back lining piece in half, pressing lightly down the fold and stitching downwards for about 8cm (3in) from the neck edge and approximately 2.5cm (1in) in from the fold. Secure the ends of your stitching carefully. Repeat the process at the hem, again stitching in 2.5cm (1in) from the fold and for about 8cm (3in) up from the hem. Do not, however, sew too far into the pleat as this will prevent it from doing its job. Most pattern instructions will also suggest a short length of stitching in the middle of the pleat around the waistline area. This is the

Centre Back Pleat of Lining

A centre back pleat or fold in the lining is a must, whether your pattern indicates this or not. This is a fold or pleat down the centre back of the jacket lining that is approximately 2.5cm (1in) deep. To cut this, place your centre back pattern piece approximately 2.5cm (1in) in from the fold of the lining fabric and cut straight out to the fold of the fabric. If your jacket pattern has a centre back seam, you can still cut your centre back lining piece with a fold, in the same way. You just omit the seam and cut the centre back piece as one. It will be much easier to make a fold or pleat in the lining piece if you cut it this way than if you try to add a fold or pleat to a shaped and stitched seam.

Jacket lining back pleat pressed into place.

best way to set the pleat but is not a problem if it is not done, in which case there could be a little more movement of the lining around the tummy area where it is often needed. Press the pleats into place towards the right-hand side of the garment and continue stitching your back lining pieces together in the same way as you did for your jacket outer fabric.

To prepare the vents in the lining, trim away the vent fabric from the centre back sides of each vent, leaving only the seam allowance. Snip into the corner that you have just made; this will allow the vent seam allowances to be pressed into place if preferred. Note that if seam allowances are pressed heavily into place before being attached and they happen to be slightly in the wrong place, it can sometimes be difficult to 'unpress' the fabric. It may be preferable, therefore, not to press the seam allowances into place, but to pin them when appropriate, stitch and then press. Either way, these will now be ready to slip-stitch to your jacket when the lin-

ing is being hemmed.

The process of making your lining is very similar to the process of making your jacket. Stitch all your lining pieces together, having made any darts required, then stitch the jacket front facing to the lining and add the jacket upper collar.

The photograph here shows the jacket from the outside looking finished, but without the lapel and the collar completed. The jacket front facing and the jacket upper collar still need to be stitched on. This will take place after they have been attached to the lining and when the lining is attached in its entirety to the jacket outer.

This is a speed tailoring or modern method of inserting a lining and is the primary tailoring method being described throughout this book. In this way you will effectively be making a full jacket, with collar and lapels, in lining fabric. Once the lining is fully made up in this way, the two garments, jacket outer and lining inner, are pinned together and machine-stitched all the way round the edge, leaving the hem mostly open to allow the jacket to be turned through. The lining hem and the sleeve lining hems are then hand-stitched in place.

Understanding this sequence of stitching is important for the speed tailoring method and makes the method of construction of the jacket and the lining much clearer. It is also quicker than traditional methods and still gives an excellent result for the home sewer.

Another result of this method is that, as the lining is made after the jacket is made, the attaching of the collar to the lining should be a little easier as it has already been completed on the jacket itself. Consider, also, that it is the collar and facing from the lining that will be visible when wearing the jacket and not the undercollar and lapel on the outer fabric, so it is good to have 'practised' on the jacket collar first!

Jacket fully stitched and ready to be lined.

Stitching the Lining Into the Jacket

Joining the lining and the jacket needs a little time and care. Starting at the collar, pin carefully and tack (baste) if necessary, working round the collar and down each side of the front of the jacket. When machining the jacket and lining together, start stitching at the collar and work down one side first, finishing at the front hem. Then return to the collar and stitch down the other side front, again finishing at the hem. As all your fabric is interfaced, it should be stable and should not move when you are sewing but sewing in stages helps to prevent fabric from 'travelling'. Your stitching will be much more successful if you sew in this way and do not try to sew all round the jacket in one go.

Stitching Collar Sections Together

This is very important because the collar will be the first focus of anyone looking at your jacket and it will be obvious if it is not sitting well. Again, the key is to take it in stages. Firstly, stitch across the outside or top edge of the collar to the first corner. Here you will have to pivot exactly on the seam allowance to ensure that an even and balanced collar is stitched on both sides. Place a pin on each corner of the collar at exactly the point where you need to finish sewing across the outside edge and pivot to sew down the side of the collar. If you insert the pin at exactly the pivot point and ignore where the pin exits the fabric, you will know to sew directly to where the pin enters the fabric. In this way, you will have much more success in turning both corners of your collar identically.

Lining made and pinned to jacket outer.

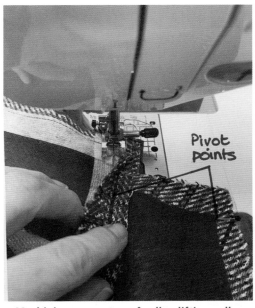

Machining across top of collar, lifting collar seam to stitch across top of lapel, with pin at pivot point on lapel.

TURNING A CORNER

When you are stitching a garment, turning a precise corner is more successful if you place a pin at exactly the point where you must pivot your stitching. Put the pin into the fabric at the point to which you will sew and then pivot. Ignore where the pin exits the fabric. Sew towards the pin entry point and stop exactly at the pin entry point to pivot. In this way you should be able to turn perfect matching corners on all your stitching. Remember when you are pivoting to leave your needle in the fabric.

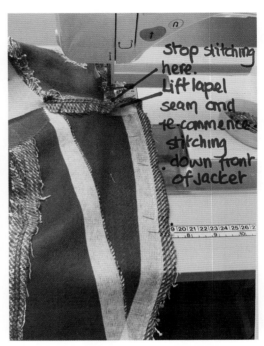

Stitching collar and across top of lapel.

Now you will be travelling down the side of the collar to the top of the lapel. Here you will find the collar and lapel seams pressed open and it can be confusing to know how to machine across these seams. From the top corner of the collar, sew down towards the lapel and pull down the seam allowance so that you can machine underneath it. Alternatively, stitch over the collar seam allowance but not the lapel seam allowance. Either way, stop stitching at the collar and lapel seam line and secure your stitches.

Once again, when pinning your jacket and lining together, if you place a pin at exactly the pivot point where the collar stops and the lapel begins, it will guide your stitching more accurately. Lift the machine needle, then lift the lapel seam allowance up and out of the way and begin sewing again across the top of the lapel, starting your stitching at exactly the point where you have just finished. From this point

onwards, you will stitch across the lapel, pivot again at the top corner of the lapel and then continue down the front of the jacket, pivoting or curving into the hem. Sew several centimetres into the hem, then stop and secure your stitching.

It is always good sewing sense to stitch seams all in the same direction, either top to bottom or bottom to top. This helps to prevent seams and fabric from 'travelling' and mismatching. Therefore, it is sensible to sew the other side of the jacket from the collar down and not to try and stitch in the opposite direction. This means that you will be sewing from the other side of your jacket, that is, from the facing or lining side. Take care to mark the pivot points accurately and repeat what you did for the first side. In this way you should achieve perfectly balanced right and left fronts to your jacket collar and lapels.

Collar and Front Facing Ease

Easing the upper collar and jacket facing is very important at this stage. The upper collar should be very slightly larger than the undercollar and the jacket facing should be very slightly larger than the jacket lapel, although the difference in them will be minimal and not easily noticed. The reason for this is to allow them to roll comfortably over when the jacket is finished and not to 'pull back' and curl up and out at the edges. If you have noticed that the collars are not quite the same size, or the facings do not match exactly, do not think that they are wrong. They need to be very slightly different in size. What you must do is to ease them together carefully when you are machining. After you have stitched them and you are pressing, you will then see how much better both the collar and the front lapels fold back.

Now it is time to turn your jacket through to the right side and check that it is all machined accurately and there are no problems with any of the stitching. Always turn your garment to the right side and 'test' it before you move on to the finishing stages and start snipping seam allowances. This applies to anything that you are stitching.

Check that the collar looks good and seems to be symmetrical, remembering that you have not yet trimmed any seam allowances, so it will not lie very well until trimmed and pressed. Have a look at the lapels and check, as best you can, that they are the same size and shape. An important point to look at is the gorge line. Make sure that there are no 'holes' in the stitching at the point where the collar meets the lapel on the front edge.

If there is a hole in the stitching, it means that the stitching stop and start points down the side of the collar and across the lapel do not match.

Gorge line on jacket with no holes in stitching.

If this is the case, then the jacket must be turned back to the wrong side and the stitching corrected. Take care if unpicking at this point. If you can, re-stitch this small area without unpicking, taking care not to change the stitching line across the lapel unless required.

Once you are happy that the jacket and the lining have been successfully stitched together, turn the jacket back through to the wrong side and begin to trim the seam allowances. Trim the collar seam allowance first, taking the corners close to the stitching without cutting through the seam line.

It may be a good idea to grade the seam allowances on the collar and lapel if your jacket fabric is on the heavy side. This will reduce the bulk inside the collar and lapel when the jacket is turned through.

Finally, snip into the seam at the break point on the lapel, again taking care not to snip

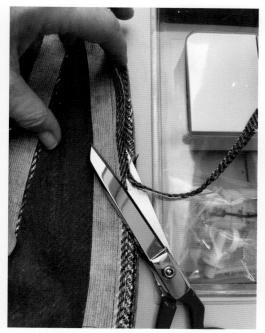

Trimming and grading seam allowances.

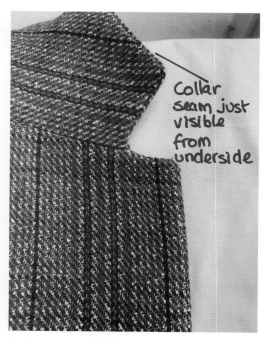

Collar seam just visible from underside

Collar pressed so that seam is not visible when wearing.

through the stitching. Doing this will help the lapel to fold/roll over better once the jacket is completed.

Pressing

Pressing will be necessary at this stage. Press open the collar seam as much as possible, using a sleeve roll. Then press the lapel seam open, again using a sleeve roll. Once this has been done, the collar, lapel and jacket leading edge must be pressed flat. At this point it is important to understand how to press the collar and the lapel. The top collar should be rolled out so that the collar seam cannot be seen when the jacket is being worn. Pressing from the undercollar side helps. Make sure that the seam is clearly visible on the side of the undercollar so that a couple of millimetres (a scant $1/8$ in) of the top

collar can be seen on the underside of the collar. Use a press cloth to protect the fabric and press with steam to set the seam. Press in small sections from the centre back of the collar out to each edge using a ham or sleeve roll if preferred. Pressing this way should help to maintain the collar shape better than trying to press the collar completely flat.

The same pressing principle applies to the lapel down to the break point. The break point is where the lapel stops on the front edge of the jacket. When the lapel is rolled back, it is again important not to see the seam running down the edge. Press from the wrong side of the lapel (that is, the side that will not be seen) and again ensure that a couple of millimetres (a scant $1/8$ in) of the jacket facing can be seen only down to the break point. Press carefully as for the collar.

From the break point, the seam down the leading or front edge of the jacket must be

Pressing lapel and front edge of jacket.

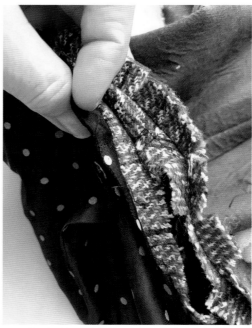

Catchstitching neck seams of lining and jacket together.

pressed to the inside of the jacket. This time press from inside the front edge of the jacket and ensure that the seam is rolled in and not visible from the outside.

Once the jacket is pressed, gently fold the collar and lapels into place and leave on a dress form or clothes hanger and allow to dry fully. It may be prudent to pin the jacket closed at this point to ensure that the collar and lapels dry in the right position.

The final step to fitting the lining and before finishing the hem is to secure the lining to the jacket in a couple of places. The first of these is at the neck edge. Going between the jacket and the lining, find the neck seams. Take the lower seam allowances of the neck edge of both the jacket and the lining and stitch them together loosely by hand. This will secure the lining to

the collar and will ensure that the collar does not 'open' up when you are taking your jacket on and off. Finally, turn the lining back down and catch the shoulder and underarm seams of the lining to the jacket with a couple of small hand-stitches. This will keep the sleeve linings in place when wearing your jacket.

Hand-Stitching the Lining to the Jacket

The jacket in the photograph here is an unlined biker-style jacket. It was decided to line the jacket and therefore the front lining piece had to be drafted from scratch. The remaining lining pieces were cut from the jacket pattern pieces.

It became clear that machine-stitching the lining into the jacket was going to be quite awkward, so the lining was fitted and stitched into place by hand. Ultimately this was quicker, more accurate and saved lots of unpicking. A hand-stitched finish definitely gives a garment the couture touch.

The lining should be carefully pinned into the jacket and then tacked (basted) in place. This will prevent the lining from moving whilst hand-stitching. It is much easier to attach the lining if it can be done on a dress form. The jacket should be placed on the dress form inside out and, after the lining has been tacked into place, a backstitch or a slip stitch should be used to carefully catch the lining to the jacket all the way round the jacket, except for the hem, as this will be finished later. Stitches should be quite close together and absolutely no further apart than 1cm (½ in). The backstitch should be very small and only just visible for the best finish; the slip stitch should be invisible. If your backstitch is very neat and secure, the lining may not need pressing and may actually be better not pressed but if using a slip stitch, the stitched edge of the lining can be gently pressed in place before the hem is turned up.

Jacket with lining pinned and tacked in place.

Jacket and Lining Hems

Hems are a sewing job that many of us would like to avoid! However, a well-turned hem will make all the difference to the final look of any garment you are making.

The jacket hem should already have been prepared with Edgefix tape before the lining was attached. Turn the hem up and pin into place. It is often a good idea to tack (baste) the hem before stitching. If this is done then place the tacking stitch along the bottom edge of the hem, close to the foldline. This will prevent the tacking stitch from interfering with the final stitching of the hem and will be easier to remove.

When hand-stitching the hem, work from left to right across the hem using a catchstitch. This stitch is slightly 'elastic' because it is a zig-zag stitch and so it will allow a little movement in the hem, preventing any pulling in the hem after it is stitched. The catchstitch will lie inside the hem (blind catchstitch) and will not be seen once the hem is fully turned up. This may seem unnecessary as the lining has still to be attached to the jacket hem and should cover any stitching. However, using a blind catchstitch inside the hem will give the best and most professional finish.

To make a blind catchstitch, fold the hem edge back enough to be able to stitch inside it. Start at the left-hand side of your work, securing the end of your thread carefully. Work from jacket to hem, catching a few threads of your jacket fabric in a right-to-left movement. Then moving to the right, take your needle up to the hem and catch a few threads from the hem in a right-to-left stitch. The stitches should be no more than 1.5cm (½ in) long at the most; if they are too long the hem will not be so secure. Move along the hem in this way and the final result should look like a herringbone stitch, similar to the photograph here. Catchstitch is very

Jacket hem with catchstitch, working from left to right.

easy and quick to do, is quite strong and is also quite flexible. Take care to ensure that the catchstitches do not go through to the right side of the jacket. Finish the hem stitches securely, hiding the final securing stitches in the hem. Remove any tacking stitches from the hem.

These instructions assume that you are right-handed. If you are left-handed you will find it easier to reverse the direction of sewing.

Hang your jacket on a dress form or clothes hanger and check the length of the lining. In theory, the jacket lining hem edge should reach the foldline of the newly hemmed jacket. However, experience dictates that linings are often not quite as tidy along the raw edge and are sometimes variable in length. If necessary, carefully tidy up the raw edge of the lining and mark how much longer it is than the jacket. The lining may need to be trimmed slightly or it may be the perfect length for hemming.

Once the lining hem edge has been tidied up, fold the lining hem allowance up so that it is about 1cm (½ in) shorter than the jacket hem. Do not be alarmed if the lining hem meets the jacket hem at the front facing. This is how is should be. The lining hem just needs to be hemmed up at a slight angle away from the front facing until it is about 1cm (½ in) shorter than the jacket hem foldline.

Pin the lining hem in place away from the hem foldline. Roll the lining back on itself and blind catchstitch the lining to the jacket hem so that when the lining is fully stitched in place, it will roll back down and the stitching will be concealed. The lining hem can be blind catchstitched in place, stitching from left to right, or a slip stitch can be used, stitching right to left, if preferred. Either way, the stitch should be invisible and slightly flexible once the lining hem fabric has been rolled back into place.

Lining hem at front facing of jacket.

Lining hem slip-stitched in place.

Hemming Round the Vent

The lining at the jacket vent is best stitched before the rest of the lining hem is stitched. Lay the jacket flat. Smooth down the centre back seam of the lining to ensure it is properly placed inside the jacket and pin the lining in place above the vent(s). Trim the lining if required and pin in place along the vent. Carefully hand-stitch the vent linings into place as shown in the photographs here.

Lining trimmed and pinned round back vent.

Lining pinned round back vent.

Lining ready to hand-stitch in place above vent.

Vents lined and finished.

BUTTONHOLES
AND FINISHING

Buttonholes on a tailored jacket, coat or waist-coat should strictly be horizontal because this arrangement holds a button more securely than a vertical buttonhole, particularly if there is any strain against the buttons, as in a neat-fitting blouse or shirt. Vertical buttonholes are often used commercially as they are quicker to make; this is because a machinist can run down the buttonhole band of a garment without removing it from the machine, making several buttonholes very quickly. For a professional finish though, it is best to use horizontal buttonholes.

Double-check that you are placing the buttonholes on the correct panel of the jacket. To start making the buttonholes, use the buttonhole guides on your paper pattern to mark the buttonholes on the front of your jacket. Alternatively, it may be that you prefer to mark your own buttonholes if you have decided to have more or fewer buttons than the pattern suggests. If this is so, mark where the first buttonhole should be, noting that it should be close to the break point. Then decide how many buttons you would like on the front of the jacket. Place them in roughly the right position on your jacket, then measure carefully between each button placement and mark the buttonholes with accurate spacing, using pins and chalk.

Machine-Stitched Buttonholes

There are three options for making buttonholes, the first being to use your machine buttonholer. If your sewing machine has a choice of buttonhole, then the one to use is the keyhole-shaped buttonholer. It looks very good on a tailored jacket and it allows the button to slip through the buttonhole more easily. The 'keyhole' end of the buttonhole should be towards the front edge of the jacket. However, if your machine has just one or two buttonhole options, choose the one you prefer and use it. Remember, whichever buttonhole style you choose, when you have used a thread colour that matches your fabric, the buttonhole will 'disappear' once it is stitched and in use.

Mark the buttonholes carefully with pins and chalk, making sure that each buttonhole is fully horizontal. Tack with large stitches around the buttonhole, keeping at least 1cm (½ in) away from the buttonhole, to secure the layers of fabric and ensure that there is no movement during stitching. Machine-stitch the buttonholes.

To open the buttonholes, place a pin directly across one end of the buttonhole and, using a stitch ripper, carefully push the blade into the

Machine-stitched buttonhole, uncut.

Choosing Bound Buttonholes

A second option is to make bound buttonholes. These are made in almost the same way as the welt pocket described earlier in the book; the difference is that the buttonhole is very much smaller than a welt pocket and so it may be more tricky to complete. The bound buttonhole is perhaps better used on a lighter fabric and not a tweed fabric. However, if you are using a tweed fabric and you would like to make bound buttonholes, then you could use either a lighter-weight contrast fabric to bind the buttonholes or you could even try using some of your lining fabric if appropriate. Binding the buttonholes with a contrast fabric would definitely move your jacket into the designer category.

If you decide to make bound buttonholes, these must be made before the jacket lining is attached to the jacket as the bindings for the buttonholes should be concealed inside the jacket and not visible on the outside.

buttonhole at the other end and slide it up to the pin. The pin will prevent the stitch ripper from going through the end of the buttonhole. Alternatively, use small sharp scissors to snip up to the pin. Trim any threads away from the buttonhole edges and any other small threads will 'felt' into the buttonhole as the jacket buttons are used.

Stitch your buttons in place one at a time, starting with the first buttonhole. Once the first button is stitched on, slip it through the buttonhole and keep the jacket buttoned in order to place the second button accurately before stitching. Continue in this way until all buttons are stitched on.

Making Bound Buttonholes

Mark the buttonholes on the front of the jacket. If the jacket fabric is quite lightweight, a small scrap of interfacing could be fused to the back of each buttonhole area to stabilize the fabric before the binding is stitched in place. Repeat the markings on the inside of the jacket, taking care to place them exactly in the same place as those on the outside of the jacket.

Cut a bias square of jacket fabric approximately 10cm (4in) square and pin it, right sides facing, to the front of the jacket directly over the buttonhole mark. Turn to the back of the but-

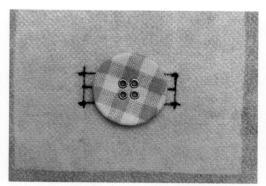

Bound buttonhole area interfaced and marked on wrong side of fabric.

Buttonhole with bias piece stitched in place (viewed from right side of fabric).

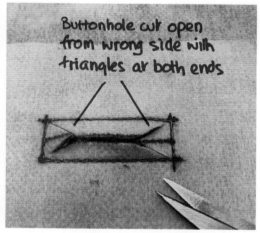

Buttonhole cut open ready to pull bias square through from right side.

tonhole and machine-stitch round the rectangle marked for the buttonhole.

Carefully cut the buttonhole open, cutting along the centre and out to each corner, making a triangle at each end of the opening.

Pull the bias square through to the inside of the jacket and ease it flat. It should look like a letterbox at this stage. Press.

Fold one side of the fabric square back onto

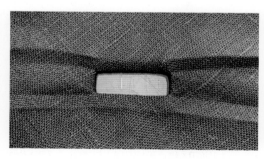

Bias square pulled through with 'lips' pressed and folded back.

Lips of buttonhole folded back ready for machining.

Stitching lips.

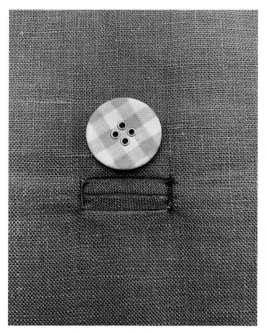

Completed buttonhole.

'Letterbox' opening for back of bound
buttonhole.

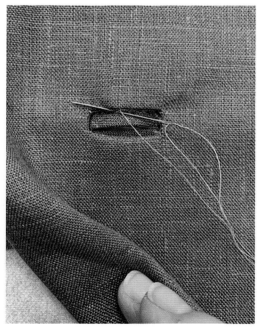

'Letterbox' opening stitched to back of bound
buttonhole.

the buttonhole opening to make a lip. Press in place. Repeat for the other side of the buttonhole. Press.

Fold back the lips and, isolating from the jacket front, secure the lips to the fabric square, one at a time, with the machine.

Repeat for the triangles at each end.

Turn to the right side of the jacket and tack (baste) the buttonhole in place until the jacket is completed.

To complete the bound buttonhole on the inside of the jacket, mark the buttonholes on the inside of the facing or lining so that they line up exactly with the newly bound buttonholes. Using a piece of light fabric, cut bias squares as above and pin to the right side of the jacket facing or lining. Machine-stitch the rectangles as above, then cut the buttonhole open and pull the fabric through until the buttonhole resembles a letterbox, as described above. Press the buttonhole flat. The facing or lining is now ready to be attached to the jacket and the buttonholes should align exactly. Once the lining has been attached and turned through to the inside of the jacket, hand-stitch the letterbox buttonholes on the facing or lining to the back of the bound buttonhole on the jacket. The photographs here show the process.

Preparing to hand-stitch buttonhole.

Hand-Stitched Buttonholes

The final option for buttonholes is to stitch them by hand. The starting point for a hand-stitched buttonhole is the same as for all buttonholes and that is careful and accurate marking on the jacket front. This is where the process is different from the machined buttonholes as the buttonhole needs to be cut open before it can be stitched. Use a silk twist or a buttonhole thread, normally a heavier thread than regular sewing thread, for the best-looking buttonhole and, if you wish, you can wax the thread before you use it; this will stop it from twisting and knotting. Beeswax or wax used for beading will work well for buttonhole work.

Mark the buttonhole accurately and then tack a wide oval around the buttonhole mark to hold the layers of fabric together whilst stitching. Then with a matching thread, tack or machine-stitch all around what will be the outside edge of the finished buttonhole, making sure that the thread is just visible. Open the buttonhole with small scissors, making sure not to cut right to each end. If a keyhole shape is preferred, use a small punch to open the buttonhole at the front edge.

If you prefer to wax your thread do it at this stage. Draw the thread across the beeswax, then place the thread in a fold of brown paper and, using a very hot iron, iron over the paper. The excess wax will transfer to the paper and your thread should stand straight. Start stitching at the right-hand side of the buttonhole, securing your thread carefully and making a bar tack. Then, working from right to left and keeping the cut edge away from you, make buttonhole stitches all round the buttonhole using the small tacking stitches as a guide. A buttonhole stitch makes a tiny knot at the top of the work if stitched correctly (as compared with blanket stitch). When working from right to left, insert the needle under the raw edge and bring the point through to the right side pointing towards you. Take the thread tail and wrap it under the point of the needle from left to right. Pull the needle and thread through and pull the latter gently away from you to finish the stitch; a knot should form along the top of the buttonhole. (If you are left-handed and working left to right, check the picture in a mirror, start stitching from the left-hand end of the buttonhole and wrap the thread from right to left.)

When you reach the keyhole end, fan the stitches out slightly, then turn the jacket and work as before to the bar tack at the end of the buttonhole. Take your needle through to the back of the buttonhole and secure the stitching carefully. Press with a hot iron and a press cloth to secure the buttonhole and to encourage the knots in the buttonhole stitch to drop into the buttonhole.

Another method of sewing a hand-stitched buttonhole is to make a machine-stitched buttonhole first. Make sure that the zig-zag width of the buttonhole is slightly narrower than the final buttonhole should be. Open the buttonhole with scissors or a stitch ripper and then hand-stitch over the machined buttonhole as described above, using buttonhole twist and taking the edge of the machined buttonhole as your stitching guide.

This method gives the security of a machine-stitched buttonhole with the lovely finish of a hand-turned buttonhole. The machine stitching acts as an excellent guide for the hand stitches.

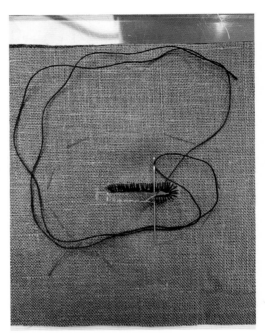

Stitching buttonhole, working right to left.

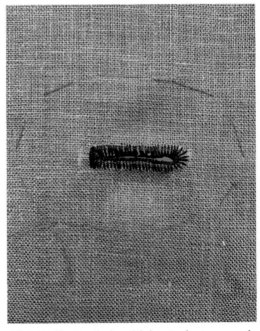

Finished buttonhole with bar tack at one end and rounded finish at keyhole end.

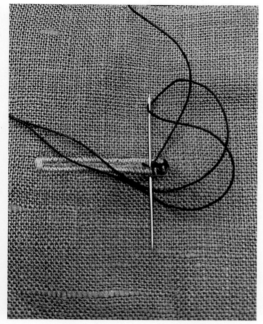

Hand-stitching over narrow machine-stitched buttonhole.

Things to Remember Before Making Buttonholes

One of the first things to remember about making buttonholes is to practise them carefully before attempting to make buttonholes on your jacket. Make sure that the fabric you practise on is the same thickness as the front of your jacket, otherwise your practice buttonholes may be perfect but your jacket buttonholes will not be as you want them.

Many sewing machines with an automatic buttonhole facility can get 'stuck' on buttonholes if the fabric is quite heavy and the buttonhole is close to the front or leading edge of the jacket. This is because the buttonhole foot moves up to the seam allowance inside the front edge of the jacket and butts up against the seam allowance and stops moving. The machine then 'thinks' that it has finished stitching and consequently the buttonhole is not properly finished. So practise, practise and practise again!

If you have any doubts at all about making buttonholes, a little tip is to take your completed jacket to a local tailor and ask them to make the buttonholes for you. They will have an industrial buttonholer that will cope with far bulkier fabric than a domestic machine can and your jacket will have beautiful buttonholes.

MAKING A CHANEL-STYLE JACKET

A Chanel-style jacket is typically round-necked, semi-fitted or with a straight hang, and sometimes slightly shorter in length. It is a classically styled jacket that suits most figure types and is therefore very popular. This style of jacket is very versatile as it can be worn casually with jeans or workwear or formally as evening dress. Choice of fabrics for this style of jacket is wide and varied and depends on the purpose of the jacket.

Historically, a true Chanel jacket has no interfacing, no lapels, has a quilted lining, chain in the hem and vented two-piece sleeves. It also traditionally has trims along pocket tops, sleeve hems and jacket front edge and hems. A great deal of the jacket is stitched by hand, including interfacings and lining, and it will have hand-sewn trim and bound buttonholes.

This chapter will describe how to make a Chanel-style jacket in a modern way that incorporates fusible interfacings and is mostly machine-stitched.

Choosing the Pattern and Fabric

As ever, this is key to a successful garment. Look at the construction lines on the pattern envelope and decide if the jacket has the construction details that you want. Is the back of the jacket cut in two or four pieces? Does the front of the jacket have princess seams or darts? How are the sleeves constructed?

Once your pattern choice has been made, the fabric and lining come next. Again, as with any jacket, the fabric choice is endless and it depends on your preference and what you want to wear with the jacket. Be sure to purchase the fabric, lining and thread all together so that when you are ready to begin sewing you will have all necessary items to hand.

Finally and before you can begin making your jacket, gather together the necessary interfacings, edge tape, bias tape, Edgefix, sleeve head and shoulder pads. Now you are ready to begin.

Getting Started

The process of making the Chanel-style jacket is exactly the same as described earlier in the book. Fabric should be prepared first by pre-shrinking to ensure no disasters at a later stage of construction or wear. It is always a good idea to make a toile or muslin to check the fit of the pattern and to make any necessary fitting or design changes before the jacket fabric is cut.

If the chosen fabric needs to be pattern-matched, then use the notches on the pattern pieces to line them up on the fabric before cutting. Take your time to lay the pattern pieces out carefully to ensure accurate pattern matching and, ultimately, a stunning-looking jacket.

Prepare the interfacing as required and then cut the jacket lining pieces. Keep all fabric, lining and interfacing pieces together with their own paper pattern piece so that nothing is lost and all pattern pieces can be quickly recognized ready for stitching. It is surprising how easy it is to mistake a side front for a side back panel on a jacket pattern!

Interfacing and Taping

Cut interfacing pieces, remembering to use the heavier of the two interfacings for the front of the jacket and the lighter interfacing for the back of the jacket and the top half of the sleeves. Trim the seam allowances from the heavier interfacing (for the front of the jacket) and fuse all the interfacing pieces to the wrong side of the jacket fabric pieces. It is not necessary to remove the seam allowances from the lighter-weight interfacing. When applying interfacing to the top half of the sleeves, trim the lower edge with pinking shears to ensure that an interfacing line does not show through on the right side of the fabric. The heavier interfacing will be used again to reinforce the shoulders and upper back and to make the shoulder plates, once some of the jacket seams have been stitched.

Using the edge tape, fuse the tape to the front or leading edge of the jacket front pieces and also to the shoulder seams on the front and back fabric pieces as described earlier in the

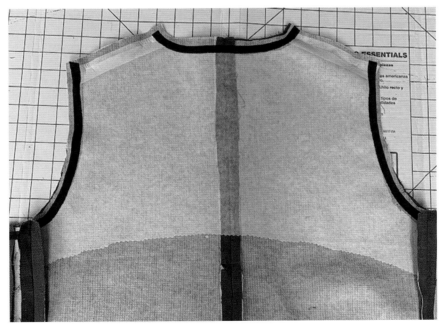

Bias tape round neck and armholes.

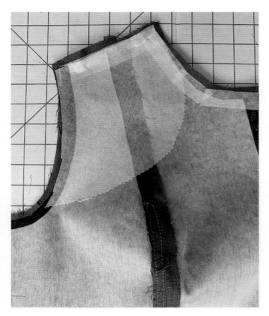

Edge tape on shoulder seam after princess seam stitched and pressed open.

book. If the jacket has princess seams, wait until the seams have been stitched before applying tape across the shoulders. The bias tape is then applied to the armhole and round the neck edge.

Remember, when fusing the tapes to the jacket pieces, to lay the tapes directly over the seam so that when the jacket is being stitched together, the stitching will go along the centre of the tapes and thus strengthen the seams.

Ready to Sew

Now you can start stitching. Start with the back of the jacket and sew the centre back seam and side back seams if present. Press all seams open. This style of jacket is unlikely to have a back vent.

Pockets

The jacket fronts should then be stitched together and seams pressed open. If pockets are to be added, they will go on at this point, before the fronts are stitched to the back of the jacket. Patch pockets are the traditional choice for this style of jacket, but welted pockets could be made at this point if preferred. Make the pockets as described in Chapter 4 and stitch in place.

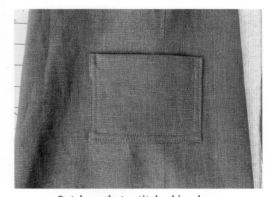

Patch pockets stitched in place.

Back Reinforcement and Shoulder Plate Interfacing

Before stitching the jacket fronts to the jacket back, some more interfacing should be applied. Using the heavier-weight interfacing, cut a piece that will fit right across the upper back of the jacket. Use the jacket back as your pattern. This piece of interfacing is the shoulder reinforcement piece and should be fused over all the other interfacing on the back of the jacket. To ensure that there is no solid interfacing line showing through from the right side of the jacket, use pinking shears to trim and curve the bottom edge of the shoulder reinforcement interfacing before it is fused in place.

The shoulder plate should now be applied to each jacket front piece. Using the jacket front as a pattern, cut two pieces of heavier-weight interfacing on the bias. Trim the curved edge of the bias pieces with pinking shears, again to prevent a line showing through on the right side of the jacket.

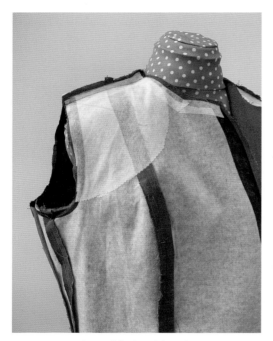

Jacket with shoulder plate.

Back reinforcement interfacing cut with pinking shears.

Sleeves – One-Piece with Dart

Sleeves on this style of jacket may be one-piece or two-piece. A one-piece sleeve will probably have an elbow dart to give the sleeve some shape. If so, make and press the dart first, then apply the Edgefix tape to the hem of the sleeve. Stitch and press each sleeve seam open.

Sleeves – Two-Piece with Vent

A two-piece sleeve will very probably have a vent opening at the cuff, usually on the hind-seam, giving the finished sleeve a smart tailored look. If this is the case, then the sleeve will be lined during the construction process and incor-

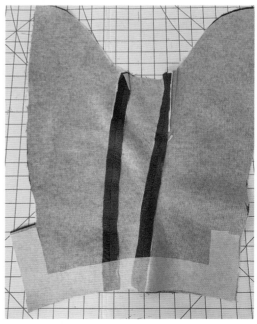

Sleeve seams stitched and hem and vent edges reinforced with interfacing.

porated into making the vent. Making a sleeve vent and lining can be daunting at first but the following steps will guide you through making a successful and beautifully finished sleeve vent.

Firstly, stitch the short or underarm seam together on each sleeve. The sleeve shown in the photograph is actually a three-piece sleeve but this is treated exactly the same way as a two-piece sleeve. In this example the short seams have been stitched and pressed open. Also note that the whole sleeve has been inter-faced as the jacket fabric is a very lightweight linen and the choice was made to interface the whole sleeve.

Once this seam has been stitched and the seam pressed open, cut a piece of interfacing to fit the bottom edge of the sleeve, as shown in the photograph, and fuse in place. This will help to produce a crisp finish to the vent.

The next step is to make the sleeve lining and attach it to the sleeve along the vent edges. Pin the lining into place and machine the vent

Lining attached to sleeve at vent edges.

Sleeve lining turned through, pressed and lining hem pinned up.

edges of the lining and the sleeve together as shown.

Snip into the corner of the vent and then turn the lining through so that the wrong side of the lining is against the wrong side of the fabric. Press carefully, then pin and tack the hems of the sleeve and lining into place.

The next stage is to sew the sleeve seams to complete the sleeve. To do this, separate the lining from the sleeve and, carefully matching the sleeve seams on the jacket fabric, stitch from the top corner of the vent, where it was snipped open, up to the top of the sleeve. Repeat for the lining seam. Press the seams open using a sleeve roll or board.

Turn the sleeve back to the right side and ensure that the top of the vent does not have any bubbles in the stitching. If it does, it may be that the snip is not quite long enough. Once you are happy with the finished sleeve, press it gently and you can then prepare to insert the sleeve into the jacket.

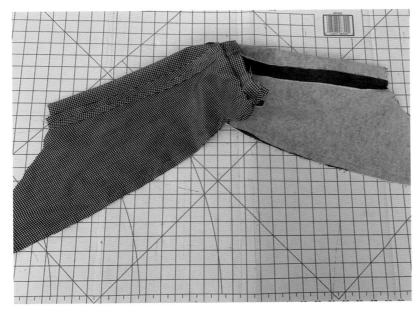

Sleeve and lining seams both stitched.

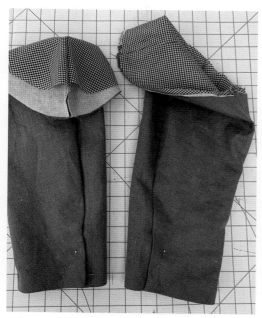

Sleeves stitched and vents pinned in place.

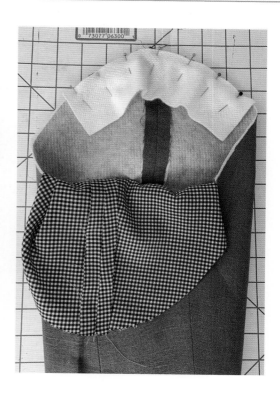

Sleeve Head

Sleeve head should now be fixed to the top of the sleeve before the sleeves are fitted and stitched to the jacket. Always remember with sleeve head to use an appropriate weight for the fabric. The jacket in the pictures here is a summer-weight linen jacket and a wool wadding has been used as sleeve head instead of a heavier purchased sleeve head. The strips of wadding are cut on the bias and stitched to the top of each sleeve before they are set into the jacket. The sleeve head should be stitched to the sleeve fabric only and not the lining.

Once the sleeve head has been attached and trimmed, the sleeves can then be fitted and stitched into the jacket. The lining should be kept free and not stitched in at this point, as it will be hand-stitched to the jacket lining at a later stage.

Sleeve head on sleeve fabric only, not on lining.

Take care when pressing the armhole seam not to press the sleeve cap/shoulder area too heavily (preferably not press it at all if possible) and do not press the underarm area either. Pressing should really only be done at the front and back of the sleeve/armhole.

Buttonholes

If you have decided to make bound button-holes, now is the time to stitch them. They should be completed before the jacket lining is attached so that the back of the buttonholes can be concealed by the lining. The instructions for making bound buttonholes are described in

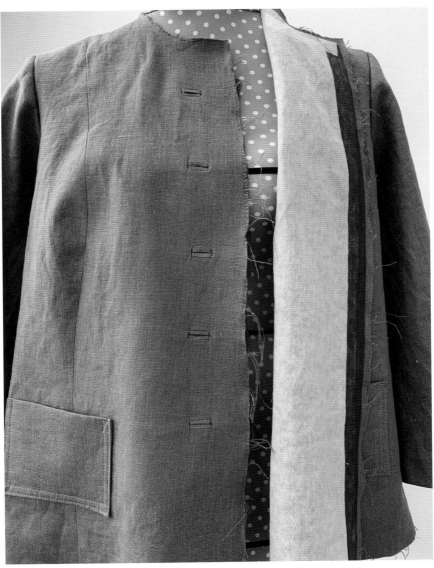

Bound buttonholes completed before lining is attached.

Chapter 6.

If you are machine-stitching or hand-stitching the buttonholes, they will be made after the rest of the jacket is finished.

Shoulder Pads

Lightweight shoulder pads make a significant difference to the hang of a jacket and now is the time to fit them if your pattern requires them. Choose an appropriate weight of shoulder pad and stitch them loosely to the shoulder seams, catching the corners of the long straight edges to the armhole seams. Take care to set the shoulder pads slightly forward of the shoulder seam, to help fill in the space below the shoulder and above the bust, and into the armhole. Push the shoulder pads out past the armhole seam until the straight edge of the pad meets the edge of the armhole seam allowance. This will help the sleeve to hang perfectly with a slightly rounded seam at the top of the sleeve.

It may be, however, that your Chanel jacket pattern does not call for shoulder pads. The Chanel jacket is typically a softly structured jacket and does not necessarily require a shoulder pad, especially if the lining is a traditional quilted lining. Therefore adding or leaving out the shoulder pad will be a matter of choice depending on how the jacket feels and looks when you put it on at this stage.

Lining

A traditional Chanel jacket has no front facing on the inside of the jacket. Therefore the lining will be made using all the jacket pattern pieces without a front facing piece. When cutting the lining for the back of the jacket a fold can be incorporated down the centre back as described earlier in the book. This would not normally be included in a traditional Chanel jacket due to construction techniques, but it can be included if preferred.

Make up the lining for the jacket, remembering that the sleeve linings are already completed and in the sleeves. Press all seams open.

If you have made bound buttonholes on your jacket, there are two options for finishing the back of them. As described in Chapter 6, 'letterbox' openings can be made in the facing or lining of the jacket. It will be essential to match them exactly to the buttonhole positions on the jacket to ensure a good neat finish and this should be done before the lining is attached to the jacket.

Alternatively, the lining can be attached to the jacket and the buttonholes marked from the front of the jacket through to the lining. Pin the jacket and lining together so that they do not move or slip and carefully mark both ends of the buttonholes on the lining. The lining can then be cut open at each buttonhole marking and the lining fabric turned in by a tiny amount and hand-stitched all round the back of the buttonhole. This method may be easier to manage as the buttonholes can be matched more easily than the 'letterbox' method described above. The finish will be just as good.

Pin the lining to the jacket round the neck edge and down each front edge. Carefully stitch the jacket and the lining together all the way round the jacket from front hem to front hem. Check and make sure that the front edges are properly matched and that the neck is crisply finished. Press the seams carefully, making sure that the lining does not roll out along the front edges of the jacket.

Turn the jacket inside out and place on a dress form if you have one. At this point it may be a good idea to stitch the jacket and lining together round the armhole with a short running stitch. This will ensure that the lining does not move when you begin to attach the sleeve

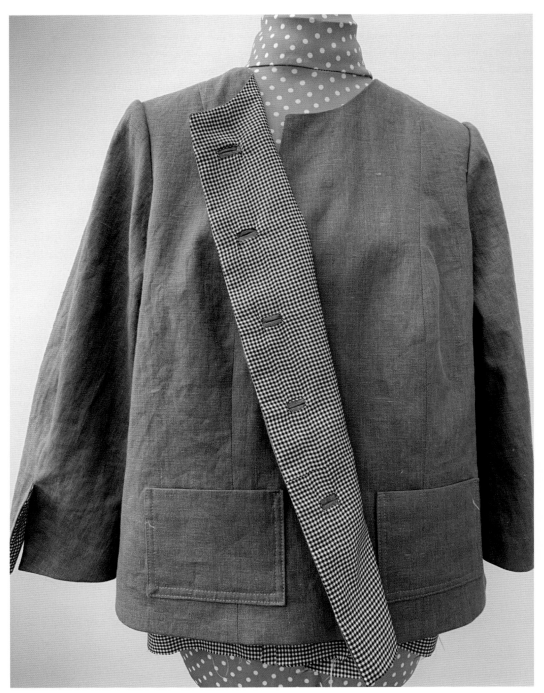

Buttonholes finished on inside of jacket.

lining.

Pull the sleeve lining up over the sleeve and carefully pin it to the armhole lining. Make sure that the armhole seam is lying out towards the sleeve, as shown in the photograph, and not turned back into the shoulder. Tack the sleeve

lining in place if necessary and secure it finally with a small, invisible slip stitch all the way round the armhole. Take care to stitch the sleeve lining to the jacket lining and not to stitch right through to the jacket itself.

Jacket turned inside out.

Sleeve lining pinned in place.

Hemming

Edgefix is now fused to the hem of the jacket if not done at an earlier stage of construction. Place the long perforations exactly where the hem will be folded up, with the wider part of the tape in the actual hem.

Finally, turn up the hem of the jacket with a blind catchstitch. Then turn the hem of the lining up and use either a catchstitch or a slip stitch to attach it to the hem of the jacket.

Finishing

If you are machine-stitching or hand-stitching buttonholes, they will be made at this stage. Carefully mark the buttonholes and complete them in the method of your choice and then stitch on the buttons.

Chanel jackets are almost always finished with a trim. If a trim is to be included on your jacket it will now be hand-stitched with matching thread and a tiny invisible stitch round the neck edge, front edges and hem.

You have now made your own Chanel-style jacket. Enjoy it and wear it with pride!

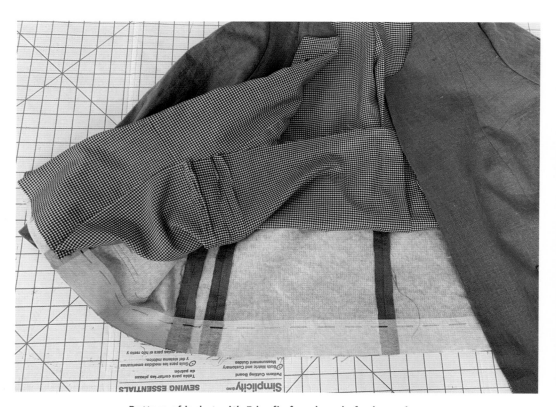

Bottom of jacket with Edgefix fused ready for hemming.

Jacket finished and ready to wear.

DESIGN YOUR OWN JACKET

You have spent a considerable amount of time learning how to make a tailored jacket using a commercial pattern and you may have made some design alterations to your jacket pattern, such as changing the length of the jacket or the sleeve, adding or removing pockets and so on. However, you can actually use a commercial pattern and re-design your jacket without having to draft a pattern from scratch.

Look for a basic jacket pattern that you like and that fits you well. Choose a pattern with a lapel as it is easier to remove a lapel from a pattern than to add one. Then decide what you would like to do with that pattern.

Although initially they look very different, the two garments shown here originate from the same basic pattern that was used to make the brown jacket. To make the blue silk tweed jacket, the collar (both upper and under) was removed and replaced by a small stand collar. The pattern pieces for the body of the jacket were extended and widened below the waist and out to the hem to make a peplum effect. And finally, the lapel points were rounded, the sleeves were shortened slightly and a wide cuff with mock buttonholes added.

The following jacket is also a remodelling of the same basic pattern.

In the pink jacket, the pattern pieces for the body panels were divided (and seam allowances added) to make a multi-panelled jacket. Again, the lower half of each panel was flared very slightly to give some shape and curve to the jacket around the waist and upper hip area. The lapel was removed and the front jacket pattern piece was extended straight up to the neck to make a collarless jacket.

The next photograph shows another Chanel-style jacket. The jacket pattern was for a casual-style, unlined jacket, but this jacket has been made in silk dupion and fully tailored for a formal finish.

What about making a fabulous tailored waistcoat! This one was made using all the tailoring techniques described in this book.

These are just some examples of what can be done with a jacket pattern and your new speed tailoring expertise. All that is needed is imagination and the confidence to try new ideas.

Be creative! Wear your jackets with pride! Enjoy what you make!

Wool check jacket.

Chanel-style jacket in silk dupion with piping.

Pink tweed Chanel-style jacket.

Back of jacket with multi-panelling and slight waist shaping.

Tailored waistcoat.

GLOSSARY

Bias tape   a narrow fusible tape, cut on the bias, for using around the armhole and neck edge of a jacket to strengthen the seams

Bound buttonhole
   a buttonhole made by encasing raw edges with fabric

Breakpoint   the point where the lapel turns back on the front edge of the jacket

Collar fall   the part of the collar that folds over

Collar stand   the part of the collar that lies against the neck

Couture   hand finished, bespoke dressmaking

Dressform   tailors dummy

Edge tape   a narrow fusible tape for using on straight edges of a jacket or other garment to strengthen the seams

Edgfix   a perforated, fusible tape used on hems, pocket tops and other areas of a garment where a crisp hem is preferred

Fusible   iron-on

Gorge line   the stitched line between the collar and the lapel of a jacket or coat

Hindseam   the longer seam on a 2-piece sleeve

Interfacing   a woven or non-woven fabric used on the wrong side of the garment fabric to add structure and body to the fabric

Lapel   the folded flap on the front of a jacket or coat

Leading edge
   the front edge of the jacket from below the break point to the hem

Mitre   a finished, angled corner on a vent on a sleeve or hem

Pivot   the point at which the direction of machine sewing changes

Princess seams
   seams that run over the bustline, from mid shoulder or armhole to waist

Rever   another name for a lapel

Roll line   the line where the collar/lapel folds over on the front of the jacket

Shoulder plate
   an extra piece of interfacing ironed onto the front shoulder of the jacket after any seams or darts have been stitched

Shoulder reinforcement
   an extra piece of interfacing ironed over the upper back/shoulder area of the jacket after centre and side back seams have been stitched

Sleeve cap/head
   the top part of the sleeve that fits into the armhole

Sleeve head   a piece of wadding stitched to the top of the jacket sleeve before the sleeve is attached to the jacket body

Sleeve roll   a sausage shaped, sawdust filled pressing tool, for using on curved seams, sleeve seams etc

Speed tailoring
   the process of tailoring a garment using fusible interfacings and tapes

Tailors ham   a rounded cushion shaped, sawdust filled pressing tool, for using on curved seams, collars etc

Toile/muslin   a fitting garment, made in calico or other suitable fabric, before making the final garment

Vent   a vertical opening on the hemline of a sleeve, coat or skirt/dress

Welt   a strip of fabric used to bind the edge(s) of a pocket on a jacket, coat, trousers etc

REFERENCES

Sleeve vents

For extra information about how to make successful vents on sleeves, jacket and skirt hems the following websites explain the process quite clearly:

www.patternscissorscloth.com

www.maledevonsewing.co.uk

MaleDevonSewing also offers an excellent tutorial on mitres

Fusible Interfacings and tapes

For full information about the use of fusible interfacings and fusible tapes, the following website is very useful:

www.SewEssential.co.uk

Welt pockets

Clear instructions for making welt pockets can be found on the following websites:

www.sfdlearningcenter.com

www.vintagesewingmachinesblog.wordpress.com

Books

Useful Reference books for home sewers include:

- Fast Fit: Easy Pattern Alterations for Every Figure by Sandra Betzina
- The complete Photo Guide to Perfect Fitting
- Tailoring: A step-by-step Guide to Creating Beautiful Customised Garments
- Couture Sewing: Tailoring Techniques by Claire Schaeffer

Magazines

Threads Magazine is an American quarterly publication available on subscription in UK. It is a magazine devoted solely to home sewers and is an extremely good reference for technical and couture sewing queries as well as for less experienced sewers.

INDEX

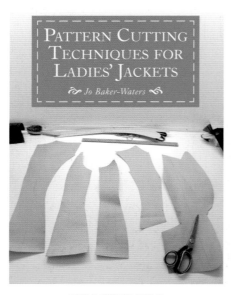

978 1 78500 177 2

978 1 78500 447 6

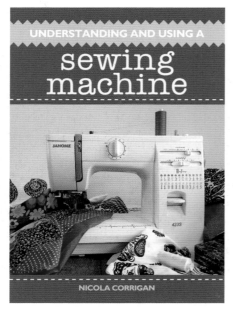

978 1 78500 499 5

978 1 84797 373 3